Tharwatul Qalb

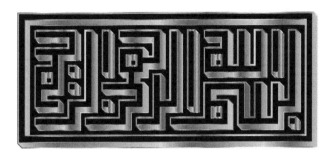

BISMILLAAHIR-RAHMAANIR-RAHEEM

The Strong Mind

Volume 1: Taking Anxiety Apart Happily, Once and for all.

Islamic Thinking meets Modern medicine
in a powerful life-changing program

Dr TK Harris MD (Oxford)
Foreword by Mufti Menk PhD (Hon)

Dedicated to all the people I have had the fortune to help
First Published September 2020, Oxford, UK

Invitation: Join my Mental Wealth Million Subs Mission.

My aim is for all the Ummah to be able to access free, effective Mental Wealth help online, in media or via books and apps.
Once my YT channel reaches 1M subcsrcribers, the platform will start paying for new projects and I can start releasing books and interactive media **free of charge.**
Please watch, subscribe and like the videos:

Find my video channel at
https://www.youtube.com/c/DrTKHarris

Donations: For those who can, please give a donation to the Mental Wealth Campaign.
Donate even $1:
Check it out at **https://gf.me/u/yp243q**

New Books, blog, latest updates:
Go to **drtkharris.wordpress.com**

Optional Audio guide: Guided audio exercises and explanations of chapters to accompany this book, available via my Etsy Store at
https://www.etsy.com/uk/shop/drtkharris

Contents

Foreword

For a long time, people have been searching for work that is drawn from combining religious teachings and medicine.

There are many such works but this one by Dr TK Harris takes it to a different level. I've known Dr TK Harris for a long while and have been following his work, integrating religion and mental health.

Unfortunately, the topic of mental health has always been subject to misconceptions in the Muslim community and our wider society as well. Some even consider it a sign of weak faith. Kudos to Dr TK Harris, that stigma is changing.

This latest work 'The Strong Mind' is a step in that direction. It's critical for people to have an understanding of Islamic psychology and how to use it as a source of strength. Why are some people weakened by difficulty while others thrive on it and are strengthened by it? The book addresses this very well! In addition, the self-tests and exercises put together give the book a good, interactive element.

We all have problems. Make an effort not to dwell on past events. Repeating in your mind negative experiences, asking "why me?" could end up with mental health suffering. Focus on the positives to offset your worries.

I fully endorse this latest work and pray that the message will spread far and wide. Many will benefit from this book and I urge those who read it to share it with family, loved ones and friends. People are suffering in silence because mental health is not discussed. Let's take the right steps to change this.

Mufti Ismail Menk
September 2020

A long, relaxed and uplifting introduction

In the name of Allah, the Beneficent and Merciful.
May his blessings rain upon the Prophet PBUH and his family,
on the Prophet Abraham AS and his family,
on all of the prophets, disciples and learned leaders of Islam,
and all the Ummah past and present.

The fact that you are reading this means you wish to gain mental strength. Tharwatul Qalb means 'Wealth of the Inner Self'.

Lesson one: just turning up and having a try is truly half the victory. May Allah bring you that strength, along with peace and contentment.

Well done for coming. Now slow down, you've come to the right place. It matters that you don't find any of this program too heavy. Treat it, and yourself, with lightness and kindness.

Lesson two: the truly strong mind is truly gentle too.

Alhamdulillah. Two of the most useful lessons in this program, already done. Let's press on!

Combining Islamic psychology theories with techniques from medicine is a much more powerful combination than relying on either one. In Muslims, the acts of praying Quran, fasting, praying salah, and tasbeeh, are all shown in separate academic studies to be of substantial benefit in helping a person's across a number of areas:
- Emotional stability
- Contentment
- Ability to experience joy and happiness
- Reduction in anger and other negative emotions

- Memory
- Attention and focusing
- Problem solving
- Greater confidence and clarity
- Self-belief without the negative self-talk
- Better relationships with others.

I could list the studies and references in here, but it would be out of place. You can find the articles and references in my blog (drtkharris.wordpress.com) if you like. This program here is not about academic proof. It is about putting the proof to use.

Islamic doctors and scientists are once again finding their voice. I have made this program with professional ethics, evidence, love for humanity and love for Allah. I have a great sense of hope and du'aa that everyone who uses this program will find benefit. Let's begin with a story.

The story of Aziz

Aziz was an engineer who loved playing football. He was a keen amateur. It helped his fitness, his friendships, and his sense of wellbeing. Once when he was playing though, he tripped over and hurt his knee. He went to see a doctor because it was very painful. The doctor said his knee would recover but he would have to stop playing football for six months, to give it time to heal.

Aziz took note of the advice but couldn't help himself. His team knew nothing of the doctor's advice and they rang him, asking if he was OK to play. Off he went to play football, in less than 2 weeks. And he hurt the same knee. Embarrassed, he saw the doctor again, who shook his head, examined him and gave him

2020 DR TK HARRIS

the news that his knee was now permanently damaged. Aziz could never play football again, and worse still, he walked with a stick. He worried that he would always need the stick.

The first time Aziz hurt his knee it was unexpected. He didn't like the news that he had to wait for six months, so he decided to go on and play. The second injury was preventable, and unnecessary.

What do we learn?
1. Difficulties befall us in life. We respond to them in various ways, sometimes good, sometimes not.

2. If we know about a problem and don't take expert advice, the consequences could be painful.

3. Strengths in one area can become weakness in another. Aziz's love for football led to a proneness to injury when he over-played and neglected to look after his body's needs.

4. At no point do we think that Aziz had a weak character or that his Deen was weak.

5. Even the second time he got hurt, nobody suggests that this was a punishment from Allah. It was simply the result of a silly decision and a bit of misfortune.

6. On hearing Aziz's story, neither you nor I thought that he had a flawed character as a person. And we know nothing about his faith or personality as such.

Aziz carried on with his life and took to careful exercises as advised. He was more mindful of the fragility of his body, and took time to thank Allah for his health. He was walking without the stick soon enough.

Now hear this story.

Five years earlier, Aziz was at University. He loved learning. One time though, he had exams coming up, and he started to worry too much about how he might pass. Normally he was a calm and generous person, but the stress was getting to him. He began to get irritable and angry. He thought that his friends were jealous of him, that they might plot against him somehow. His best friend convinced him to see a doctor, who diagnosed anxiety disorder and suggested that he take some time at home, and delay his exam until the next term. He also prescribed Aziz some tablets.

Aziz understood, but didn't want to fall behind. He stayed at university, skipped the tablets, and tried to pass his exams. In the end, he failed, and his mind suffered more. His parents took him home, and it was another whole year before he recovered. He had to take slightly stronger pills than the ones he refused before.

What do we learn?
1, 2 and 3: the same lessons as above.

4. Be honest. Some of you will already be thinking now that Aziz is a bit of a maniac. He was studying too much, and it was no surprise she got a bit crazy. Who knows what he would do next?

5. Some of us will also think maybe someone put a spell on him. Or that he should pray Quran more, letting go of his books.

6. Some of us would form negative views about his character. Who is so weak as to get paranoid and lose their mind when stressed? Who would freak out so much over exams?

In the end, Aziz followed the advice of his doctor and made more

Get Videos & Books, Raise Funds drtkharris.wordpress.com

time for his mind. He slowed down deliberately, perform his salah in a far more relaxed and mindful way, rather than in a sense of hurry. He took more time for recreation: this is actually how he got into football! His mind found its health again and he got his first job after graduation- as an engineer.

- **Character attribution:** Do we associate a mental health condition to be a result of a deeper flaw than a physical one?
- **Stigmatisation**: Would we feel more confident with Aziz when he had a knew problem, and keener to show him understanding and support, compared to when he was struggling mentally?
- **Religious inference:** Do we tend to think more of religious causes for mental health issues, whereas physical issues are just purely physical: no religious causes or concerns to be had?

Looking at Aziz's stories in another, more balanced light, we find something interesting. A love for football becomes a risk of injury. A love for learning becomes a fear of failing. We make bad decisions when we are clouded by emotional judgments. Our task is to train our minds to spot the signs and deal with the issues, and inshallah, use sense, step by step methods, and ask Allah for help. Treat the mind as you would any other body part: try to under stand it, and look after it both when well and when ill.

And so we come to understanding that we should view mental health as a matter of strengths and abilities which sometimes lose their balance and become problematic. In some cases, problems both troublesome and helpful, depending on your view. Read on.

Every problem happens in a *dynamic situation* in life, meaning that different forces push and pull the problem. People rarely suffer in a bubble: the benefits and drawbacks of their issues are felt both by the person and those around them.

Take this situation, which I am sure many of us will recognise.

Amreen is a worrier by nature, and she knows it. At 50, mother of three boys, she is always concerned about safety, order, and acting within the bounds of social acceptability. She is always cleaning, preparing, and making sure the house is stocked and up to scratch. On the surface, she comes across as very house proud.

She was always a shy person and tends to avoid mixing with the other mothers for fear of coming across as naive. She is a stickler for cleanliness and neatness. Her anxiety makes sure she picks up on social situations more quickly than them, knowing what people's reactions and emotions are up to.

 The family have relied on her habits, and not made a huge fuss about forcing her to go to see a doctor. They silently think that if she wasn't anxious and proper, they would have to do a lot more work around the house.

As young boys her sons were spoiled because she would make sure their rooms were tidy to the point of looking immaculate: she prefers to do the tidying herself rather than leave her 'rabble' to do it.

The dynamics can be considered in terms of *gains*.
Having the anxiety disorder is troubling for Amreen. But she does gain something: her inner instinct for caring for her family is served by the disorder

Her family are upset to see her struggling. But they gain

Get Videos & Books, Raise Funds drtkharris.wordpress.com

something. Their inner instinct to be looked after and have a life of ease is served by her disorder too.

Her anxiety makes her exhausted, but he is kind of stuck with it because it has been her reluctant ally, a tool which has been helpful to her in proving her worth as a mum. She hasn't quite realised the strength of this inner force.

Seeing a counsellor once helped her vent her frustrations and try the occasional technique to reduce the anxiety and relax more, but she couldn't keep up this change. It's as if the old habits return because they are familiar ground. There is always comfort in familiarity, even if it is unpleasant. This principle alone keeps many people stuck in a rut.

She prays to Allah every salah, asking to be free from anxiety. She hasn't made the connection.

So. Is there a third way? Is there something that can help Amreen to live with the benefits of her anxiety—order, safety, neatness-without the negative sides: exhaustion, aches and pains, and increasingly in old age, arthritis, high blood pressure and gut trouble? How can she feel less troubled? What kind of du'aas should she pray? What should her aim be? To be free from worries, or to live with them better? What conversations should she be having with her sons about her issues? Would'n't it be a good idea for them to help her out?

If you can relate to Amreen or Aziz or their families and loved ones in any small way, this program will give you plenty to build your mind up strong and successful. The answers are different for every person, so I can't tell you what will work for you. But because this program asks for your own input, you will unearth the treasure for yourself. It was always in you; I will just show you ways how to find it, inshallah.

Allah has given you all you need, both inside you and outside

This program is about finding the strengths in you that were already there. It is about confirming your belief in yourself, in Islam. Reduction in anxiety and worries is almost like a side effect of this bigger mission. You have every reason to feel very optimistic and certain that you will emerge wiser, less conflicted about what works for you. Just turn up and try, that's all you need.

You will examine the breadth of your wonderful inner character, and examine all the things that you are: your apparent positives, your apparent troubles. Recognise that getting on top of them means understanding yourself properly. Once you do this, you will find that the issues you face can be firstly understood, then made less troublesome, and then even turned to your advantage, to strengthen you.

If you have doubts, let me allay them here. Allah has promised us this:

> 'Allah does not burden a soul more than it can bear'
> (Quran 2.286.)

If you feel broken, know that this is just a *feeling*: feelings are not facts. I *guarantee* that you are not to be broken: Allah has made you unbreakable. He has said so, right in that quote. And look at the next quote:

> 'And whoever relies on Allah- then Allah is sufficient for them.
> Allah will accomplish Allah's purpose for them.
> He has set everything within its (time and) limits.'
> (Quran 65:3)

So, you have been set things in your destiny, and Allah has made you with a purpose. And if you are a believer, you must know that he loves you, far more than you could even love yourself. He believes in you. He says so, right up there. Hang on to that, and use it. It is power; it is fuel and certainty that you have every right to rely on.

Examine your anxiety, or any other difficulty or insecurity, and know that it is neither friend nor foe: it is simply there, and you can become acquainted with it in order to manage it better. Every effort you make will pay off in a small way, bit by bit, building you back up. This is a continuous and steady process, and as you do it, your greater self awareness and greater contentment will make you feel more masterful in life and closer to Allah than ever, inshallah. What greater wealth is there than mental wealth?

Islam's view of difficulties and problems

Water is useful when we are thirsty and drink a cupful, but if we drank a lake it wouldn't serve us well. Fire is useful to warm and cook, but we wouldn't heat our food in a raging forest inferno.

Alhamdulillah. This is what Allah has told us from the beginning. Whatever it is, good or bad on the surface, there are hidden benefits or risks associated with it. It depends how you handle it.

Allah has made us all differently for reasons of his own, but we are learning the reasons over time. We are not designed to be independent as a species, each person living their own exclusive life. We are, instead, designed to be a social, *inter-dependent* species, relying on each other, each with our own particular strengths and weaknesses, forming a collective that is far stronger than our individual features.

To that end, Islam offers us a perspective when it comes to health problems and difficulties of any kind: they should be seen as neither good nor bad, but simply as tasks, exercises and opportunities. We all know the negatives of being unwell or mental disorders.

Could it be that the 'disorder' was originally some kind of solution that just got out of hand? Let's do something brave and think if there are possible benefits to illness:

1. Protection from further harm.
An illness may be a short term reaction to a situation that actually protects you from further harm. If someone got injured doing something risky, anxiety disorder might be a protective and useful device, in the short term, protecting them from getting back out there too quickly.

2. Binding, loyalty, and unity.
The process of helping each other through difficulty is essential to the process of bonding. It is, perhaps, a crucial advantage to have a society where people depend on each other: they forge stronger loyalties, and the gratitude of people who receive help is repaid when they are better. Social health can be improved by caring for individual ill health.

3. Growth through solving problems.
Having pain or problems is the main motivation why many of us get out and seek knowledge. We exist to solve problems, and we are more motivated when those problems are at risk of harming us of the people we love. What greater and more noble pursuits are there than helping a fellow creature of Allah?

4. Specialisation and diversity

For example, insomnia (being unable to sleep) is a problem for one person, but it could also be the thing that leads that person to save his family.

How? What fresh madness is this, I hear you ask? Imagine two separate families. One has an insomniac, the other doesn't. If a group of marauders came along, which house would be more likely to spot the danger and defend itself? That's right. The one with the poor soul who is awake.

It is true to say that the person themselves may not find the problem pleasant, but the burden they carry has an advantage for them and their family. So imagine asking an insomniac, who saved his whole family from being killed, if he was glad in the end that Allah gave him the disorder?? Of course he was.

It is not about avoiding problems in life: it is about how you bear them, that separates the strong minds from the fragile. Both strong minds and weaker ones face the same number of issues, on average. The good news is that everyone can gain a strong mind: it doesn't depend on intelligence, or genetics, or anything. It depends on the willingness to try.

5. An adaptive benefit.
Sickle cell anaemia is a type of disorder which is very painful and disabling, especially in the cold weather. Blood vessels get narrow, and the blood can't get through because the blood cells get a distorted shape Extremely uncomfortable. But the very problem is why people with the disorder are resistant to malaria: the distorted shape makes it difficult for the malaria parasite to enter the blood cell. So we find the disorder more commonly in hot countries where malaria is a problem. And so it is with many issues that afflict us. Not all, but many diseases are the result of adaptations that are in the wrong place at that moment.

17

Why do some people get weakened by difficulty, and others strengthened by it?

It depends how bad the difficulty is, what the situation was, and what approach the person takes, and if there were benefits from the difficulty, both known or unknown.

Pain and suffering are part of life. Life hurts. Going through difficulty can and does give some people meaning and motive to carry on, even improving them. A period of illness can cause a previously cold or detached person to re-evaluate their life and be more compassionate. A mother's sickness can bring a warring family together, setting aside their petty prides and bickering to see what the real meaning of life is about.

But equally, illness can foster bitterness, damage someone's welfare or ability to enjoy life, and brings the worst out in people who would otherwise be far nicer and more compassionate if they didn't have a constant battle with illness.....and so on.

Balance is more truthful than mindless obsession with just the positives or negatives of a situation. Being lost in negativity is harmful, and so is being lost in positivity: life is not kind to those who just see positives without sensing dangers.

Balance is truth, and in finding that balance we have the key to better stability.

How we treat ourselves and others: The meaning of Islam

True strength is found in understanding what we can and cannot control, being patient, and submission to the tools and tasks that Allah has given us. This is also, quite poetically, the true meaning of Islam.

'Difficulties can make you better, or bitter. You can choose which.'
-One of Mufti menk's many quotes.

Part of Islamic psychology is the principle of kindness to oneself, and respect for one's own dignity. This includes how one treats other people. If someone you loved had a boss that bullied them at work, would you think that was OK?

Once, Sarah was standing in front of people talking about something. She prepared well, but still, she forgot her lines a little bit in the middle of her speech, and found her self muttering under her breath 'Idiot!'. Would that actually help her to get the speech done properly? Of course not. Would Allah or the Prophet PBUH talk to Sarah like that? Of course not. Sarah had no idea she had such a dim view of herself.

Kindness to people includes yourself. If you swear at yourself or are harsh and abusive in the way you view yourself, you are mistreating one of Allah's creatures! Perhaps it's an idea to be kinder. We will, after all, be asked to account for our actions.

The internal voice is a bit like your inner boss. He (or she) reflects what you want to do, and comments on how well you do stuff or not. Many of us have a bit of a crappy inner boss. Maybe we should be kinder to ourselves by firing them, or demanding that they are more encouraging and kind? Such a boss would bring the best out in us.

If you have struggles right now, be kind to yourself. Accept that it is hard. It is not a sign of weakness; it is a sign that you are struggling, that's all. You are right, and not alone: life is very difficult, for many people. The strongest muscle-bound man can be totally terrified of a little needle.

Knowledge alone is enough to fix many a problem

Some parts of this program are just facts or information. Your brain will know what to do with them: trust it. Just take the facts and digest. Make the odd note, think about the issues, reflect on them, discuss them with a friend or relative. Repeat the reading, because while our brains are fantastic, memory is treacherous: it always needs repetition to make your knowledge solid. Solid knowledge itself is part of effective treatment.

How so? Well, because once you know about something, your own intelligence and wisdom can see how the useful new facts can enrich your life and move you forward. You must believe in your own *agency:* that knowing the facts leads you to your own sensible solutions.

Let's have an example. Imagine you came to me saying 'Doctor Harris, I've been feeling too hot over the last 2 weeks. I might be coming down with something. Can you help?'

I ask you questions, do some tests. You tell me that you fear it might even be contagious: other family members have also felt feverish recently. I take some samples, then leave you in the room for a while, and then I come back. I tell you what I have found.

"It seems as if you have turned your heating up too high at home. It is set to 40 degrees celsius." I say.

You don't need advice as to what to do next. You know what to do. And even before the problem is fixed, you feel the relief just from knowing.

Get Videos & Books, Raise Funds drtkharris.wordpress.com

Giving thanks

Before going on, I want you to remember to thank Allah for giving you whatever problems you have. After your next salah, pray 2 rakats Nafl salah, at a slow pace, with grace and comfort, as if you were really on your best behaviour, with not a care in the world other than to impress Allah with how grateful you are to Him.

Then, when in sujood, spend some time telling Allah about how deeply grateful for this chance, and fully energised about building yourself up to have a strong Muslim mind and heart. No pain, no gain. You will try, with good cheer and with as light and humble a heart as possible. Nothing is easy, but this program is very do-able. Everything here is very do-able, I promise you that.

The goal of this program is to help all of us, whether you suffer from anxiety or not, and regardless of whether you are also getting help from a professional. If you have success using the techniques presented here without the help of a professional guide, good for you! But if you still find yourself struggling after trying the techniques, don't give up. Seek outside help.

Make du'aa and say Bismillah before embarking on anything. Adopt a relentlessly positive attitude: after all, the Lord of all creation is with you on this mission. Always, always have faith that Allah will help.

Don't bother with a session if you feel totally unmotivated or too terrified to read it. A little bit of apprehension and self-doubt is fine, because it gives you a spark of energy. But not too much. Don't let the program become another symbol of what you can't do. Take it as a collection of ideas and chances, a large collection of positive notes.

NEVER read or do the program because you feel you 'have to', like it is a chore and burden itself. It is not yet another thing to burden yourself with. It is a toolbox, not a torture device.

ALWAYS come to it with a sense of curiosity, positiveness, and reassurance that every second you spend on it is a reward from Allah. Why the reward? Because you are making the effort to be your best. That is all Allah ever asks of us.

Dr TK Harris
Muharram 1442 AH
September 2020

.. and a thank you for buying.
Finally, thank you so much for buying this. You are helping a great cause. My mission is to one day bring simple mental health access to all Muslims anywhere, free of charge inshallah, via online media, free publications and voluntary work. We must help each other as a whole to do our best; to be citizens who have goodness and dignity running right through us, and prove ourselves worthy of the Muslim name.

If you want to help more, go to our Gofundme page (search online or get the link from drtkharris.wordpress.com to donate whatever you like towards making this ambition a reality.

Get Videos & Books, Raise Funds drtkharris.wordpress.com

Welcome to reclaiming your mind, inshallah!

Aims of this section:
- Understand what attitude works well for this program.
- Recognise the 5 main points of 'mental wellbeing'.

Dear reader, you need not fear anything. The fact that you have turned up to read these words already puts you ahead. Have you said bismillah? Good. Commence every new and noble effort with the name of Allah.

Now it is simply a matter of trying your best, slowly and experimentally. You need not get it right first time, or even second time. When you were a baby, could you walk perfectly the first time you tried? No. Did it stop you? No. And you were just a baby back then! So keep trying gently and persistently. Don't exhaust yourself, try to see it as a positive thing. Take time to laugh at yourself, find the good humour in not getting it right. Greet issues with good cheer. Even if you don't feel happy, force a smile: Allah is with you, nothing can get in your way if Allah rewards your efforts as you wish. Plus it is scientifically proven that forcing a smile and breathing gently in and out actually tricks the brain into happy feelings after as little as three minutes.

How do I know that the methods are actually working?

1. The benefit of scientific research. The scientific evidence for these methods is vast, and clear: they are effective in helping people.

2. Scores and numbers. You will be rating yourself through little quizzes and questions, as you go along. You will see your knowledge and confidence grow, and troublesome issues will get less.

23

3. Even right now, the process is working. By reading and writing anything to do with the program, you are putting your mind in a special place: thinking logically, accessing calmness, and treating the issues at hand with a sense of detachment and confidence. Every second you spend even trying to do this, is excellent news. It's like digging for gold: you think you are looking for the gold, but in the meantime, you become fitter, you learn about the earth, and you gain peace from doing something constructive and productive. It doesn't even matter if you don't find gold: you have already improved your life by choosing something worthy to do.

This program, and in fact the whole aim of any treatment, is not to remove worry and anxiety altogether. (*Note: I will use the two terms 'anxiety' and 'worry' interchangeably*).

Anxieties are part of normal psychology in everyday life. Our emotions and Nafs are essential to our life just as much as much as it is important for a car to have safety features like brakes and an alarm.

Worries are mostly exaggerated and misleading. Don't fall for fake news inside your own head. The trick is to recognise it and use the part of it that might be helpful: you can never get rid of fake news, but you can learn to deal with it effectively.

It is unwise and unrealistic to expect that you will be some blissful 'worry free' person. This is only promised to us in Jannah (paradise). In this world, having worries and stresses is part of our fundamental experience. The point, and the aim, is to have them at a manageable degree, where you can experience a balance of emotions and have the ingredients for good wellbeing. Solving problems can be and is a source of great joy and satisfaction on occasion.

I call this my 'wellbeing box':

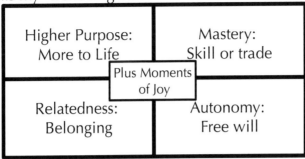

These are the things that any person should be able to have in terms of the ingredients for contentment. These issues are covered a lot in my book Instant Actions but they are not directly connected to mental illness as such. They are easier to have if you don't have a mental disorder, that's all.

Even now your mind might be trying to interfere with your reading, but that's OK. If and when the time is right, Allah will bring you the right moment and slowly but surely you will succeed. It is already written in your life story. You have tolerated your struggles this far, and now you are on the verge of finding solutions.

Every single thing is known to Allah, and if you are suffering, every moment will be known to Him too.

Why combining Islam with medicine is important

Aims of this section:
Learning how Islamic knowledge blends seamlessly with modern 'growth psychology'.

This program isn't about diagnosing what disorders we might have. That's the job of professionals. It is about understanding ourselves better, trying to overcome mild or moderate issues on our own or with a friend to help out, and knowing when to call for outside professional help. It is also about knowing how mental wellbeing and strength can be supported by Deen. Mental health issues are not a sign of weak character or weak Deen, no more than having trouble with your joints or your heart is an indicator of your character as a person.

On the contrary: mental health issues are particularly amenable to relief and contentment if you seek the refuge and wisdom of Deen and faith in God. Many people with mental health issues are in fact very faithful and hopeful when they are well, and it is therefore especially distressing for them to feel their faith under attack when they have a mental health problem. When they emerge from the problem, their faith may be weakened if their symptoms included worries that Allah may have abandoned them, or loss of a sense of meaning to life. What a terrible loss! Loss or weakened faith is a possible consequence of the damage that mental illness can cause. This is preventable and urgent. If not, it is associated with poor functioning in the longer term.

It is urgent that people have the right guidance as to how to see the issues at stake, and how to use Islamic psychology as it has always been intended: a source of strength. This is why it is ever so important to be sensitive to religious matters when mental health issues crop up.

People can emerge stronger than ever after treatment, with the right approach. Such people can live lives with greater meaning and purpose than ever before, as if the illness put them closer to Allah and renewed their sense of how precious life is. Many a great achiever has only emerged after a period of suffering. I have helped and coached some exceptionally successful sportspeople, entrepreneurs and other professionals who only discovered and followed their passions in life after a period of such illness. The evidence bears it out: in those who achieve exceptionally highly, there are higher rates of background mental illness.

This issue is called post-event spiritual growth, and is very real, and we have ways of encouraging it to happen, and in helping maintain the wellness once it returns, alhamdulillah.

Most people will not be 'transformed', but will be very happy and glad to return to a state of contentment and normality. It is a harrowing experience to have your mind suffer. Even if one does not emerge 'transformed', it is still a distinct advantage to have religion. As stated in the beginning, it is a proven fact through many studies, that those with beliefs in a God have better mental health, lower rates of suicide, and better coping with trauma or unexpected adverse events. Subhanallah.

How do I work with this book?

Aims of this section:
- *To understand how to read the knowledge parts of the book*
- *To understand how to approach the quizzes and tests.*
- *To consider who could help you, if anyone*
- *To understand the attitude of faith and optimism*

There are different strategies in the book. All of them require some gentle effort to be put in.

Some parts are just reading and reflecting on what you read. But I want you to practice **active reading.** This is a relaxed process which improves memory and understanding vastly. You have all the time in the world. Respect yourself, don't rush.

The steps are Skim, Ask, Read, Remember, Skim. *S.A.R.R.S.*

1. <u>Skim.</u> Before you read any chapter, have a skim of it, for a couple of minutes. Note down the odd sentence or phrase. Just get a vague idea. I have helped you by putting the aims at the beginning of many such chapters.

2. <u>Ask. Then ask yourself a few questions: what do you want to know from that chapter?</u>, and how would that knowledge relate to your situation?

3. <u>Read.</u> Read the chapter through; scribble the useful sentences or points in the margin, on the page, or highlight the things that stand out as new and helpful. Stop to ponder a point if it intrigues you. If something seems confusing; leave it and just go to the next point.

4. <u>Remember:</u> Once read, close your eyes and try to remember 5 main points about what the chapter was about, and why it would help you.

5. <u>Skim.</u> Have a skim of the chapter again to shut down and fix your memory.

Doing this helps your memory and motivation. The knowledge is far more likely to help you out. This method is in fact useful for anything you want to read and learn. As you get better at it, you get far quicker too inshallah.

<u>Interactive questionnaires</u>

Bits of information, and points of learning, will lead to tests quizzes or questionnaires that are designed to help you learn in more detail about both the condition and yourself.

Many of the exercises will have a repeated element, a bit like exercises in the gym, or antibiotics: one dose is not enough, and you need to return and repeat them in order to

1. See how well you are doing compared to before.

2. Learn the important facts once again.

3. Gain a picture of how you are over time, and how you might even interpret the questions differently the further you go along.

4. Refresh and deepen your knowledge and faith in yourself and Allah. Example: Nobody reads the Quran just once: we repeat the same lessons, even the ones we think we know, because they find a deeper place in our hearts with each repetition.

Other parts ask you to add thoughts of your own. You might need to fill out a quiz, write your ideas down, and check in with certain things once a week. Think of it as a mental gym: you come here to work out.

If you can, try to master each technique before moving on to the next strategy, even if this means you spend several weeks working on just one type. If this isn't working out at all, then that's OK, skip ahead.

Not all strategies will work out for everyone. They will all be a little bit hard: after all, you are conquering a difficult problem. Very few great problems are overcome easily or at once, but they can be overcome gently and calmly.

 How often should I work on the exercises?

Try to stick to a regular schedule. Most exercises are suited to about half an hour: steal the time and put it into your day, your calendar, your phone, or make a reminder chart on your wall with days marked out. If you see the serious people in the gym, they walk around with a little notebook, or noting their progress on a device. Measuring and recording is how victory will be mapped out, and it is especially useful in mental health, where progress is not visible on the outside immediately.

Unlike the gym though, this book doesn't need you to be dressed up in spandex or anything ridiculous like that! You can ease into it like a warm comfortable pool, taking it in slowly and steadily.

Everyone has their own 'cosy time' when they can take a few moments to themselves with a cup of tea and some peace. Find yours. Perhaps after Fajr or during a half hour or so of peace at lunch time or evening. Make it in a comfortable place. Mark the work off on a scheduler or calendar. For any given exercise, pick a regular time and place for working once a week, maximum twice a week, for about 1 hour a session. There are some smaller exercises that you can do every day.

Reclaim some confidence in yourself: Allah put it there.

Allah gave you a great Intellect in there. (Imagine me pointing at your head).

I will show you the guidance, the road map, but you must walk on this journey. You are also a sensible, intelligent person with your own mind. Practice using it. You can decide what works for you. Nobody is a machine, and nobody knows everything. You might get it wrong, but that's totally fine. You'll find your own way, inshallah. It starts here, now. The present moment is a great gift Allah has given us, so let's just move with it.

'Who will help me?'

Allah himself of course. Ask Him and He will come. He will help your brain to find the solutions and wisdom that float above all difficulties. You put in the work and du'aa, and Allah provides the relief and eventual cure.

Anyone else?
Do involve someone else if they are willing and you are inclined. They can help by:
Love and support:
A loved one knowing you are doing this can give you that gentle touch, that extra confidence and support even if they are not directly involved.

Relating:

If you find someone who has a similar issue and decide to work together, that helps with motivation and making sure you turn up to 'sessions' you have scheduled. Some people use this book to work with a therapist.

Administrative support:
If you are scatter-brained, don't despair. Ask someone to ring you or remind you when you are due to do a session, or to help you fill out the quizzes if you struggle with writing your thoughts. Use your phone as a reminder device if you like.

Another person is not totally essential unless you are in a severely impaired mental state and can't even focus for a second. If you feel OK with trying things out yourself, then go right ahead. If it's too much, then make a Plan B and get some outside help. Even a relative or friend to remind you to do your exercises will help, as will setting reminder alarms on your phone.

When Should I See a Professional?

This program can be considered a *low-intensity tool*. It's an ideal tool for people whose anxiety symptoms are mild to moderate: you can still manage most of your daily activities and concentrate enough to work through the steps in the workbook. While they cannot be considered 'formal medical advice' they are drawn from good evidence and can work as well as seeing a professional.

If you find yourself at risk of bringing harm to yourself or someone else, then please seek help. If you have tried to work with the program but just can't, having tried and tried over several days, then call for outside help too. There is no shame in this. Just as a top athlete will do exercises to build up a weak muscle, he knows that if it's too painful he will see a doctor. This is NO different.

To find people who can help, there are often many state or privately funded mental health support organisations. Just search online and you may well find a support group or online forum with plenty of tips and helpful people.

Remember also the religious support: many local A'lims and muslim leaders have a prime function in helping support many people through difficult times. They are confidential, but if you know them personally or feel awkward, then you could try ringing one outside your area for more anonymous support. Do anything that makes sense to you.

Whether you do it yourself, or with someone else, and whether you find yourself slipping backwards or not, remember that Allah will always be there. Talking to Him, asking for His help, at any time day or night, is a habit you must forge. When you talk to him, don't do it out of desperation: do it with optimism, positivity and hope in your heart. Allah loves it when people really act like they have total faith He will help them out. But in the end, even if you can't muster that positivity, offer whatever you can by way of asking for his help. We are fragile earthly beings after all, and Allah knows our pain and our hassles very well.

After all, if you pray to Allah asking for anything, one of these three things is guaranteed to happen:

a) He grants your wish now or very soon
b) He gives you something else which will serve you better
c) He grants you the wish later in life or in the hereafter.

You cannot lose if Allah is on your side. Faith is an extremely powerful psychological device, and God has power over all.

Seeing a professional
Anxiety disorders can be treated by a wide range of mental health professionals, most typically psychologists, clinical social workers, and counsellors. Although all psychiatrists (medical doctors who specialise in mental health) and most family doctors will prescribe medication for anxiety, and may even give you some brief anxiety management advice, they are usually focussed on helping patients with medicines and ways other than talking therapy.

Clinical psychologists and psychotherapists come in here. They are not medically qualified: if they are called doctor, it is because some of them have PhDs- a respected academic doctorate, not a medical doctorate. As a broad umbrella term, most of them don't mind being called 'therapists' as a profession. They do excellent work.

To find a good one, it is a matter of doing some research. It is still legal for a person to set up in business as a 'counsellor' in most countries without any qualification as such, so unfortunately this means many people claim to be therapists without the extent of training or experience that would help them to remain professional. Most reputable therapists belong to a recognised organisation. In the UK, we have the UKCP and the BACP which most therapists will have a membership. You can search their member lists online.

Online therapists

Internationally, many more therapists nowadays will work with patients abroad due to the advent of effective online meetings. This is a good option for many people, but be extra careful: if something goes wrong, for example you feel mistreated or the clinician makes a damaging mistake, there is often not the kind of insurance coverage or regulatory body who can offer to intervene if you get poor treatment. Regulatory bodies rarely work across international boundaries. Do as much research as you can, and remember you can always withdraw from treatment if you don't feel safe. Avoid paying for therapy upfront from the beginning if you can: better to see how a couple of sessions go first and agree on a limit to the number of sessions in total.

The main sense of whether therapy is going to work for you is the quality of the bond you form with your therapist: you should feel positively regarded, trusted, and able to talk about things with them as freely as anyone you have ever met. They, by return, will look to set boundaries with you as to when and where you can speak, and they will probably work to identify 'themes' or specific problems to work on, so that you don't end up talking without any specific purpose. The exception is psychoanalysis, which is a different type of therapy not readily suited to limited sessions, or aims and outcomes as such.

Medication

Medication is often used alone, but it works better if used in conjunction with psychotherapy.

Medication	Advantages	Disadvantages
Antidepressants including citalopram, venlafaxine, duloxetine, mirtazapine etc. Prozac, Zoloft, SSRIs, SNRIs etc.	Helpful long term especially if depression also present. Effective against OCD too Not addictive.	Take more than 2 weeks to start working. Might be difficult to come off because of some side effects on stopping.
Benzodiazepines (diazepam, valium, etc	Very good short term; quick acting.	Sedating. Addictive and damaging in the long term beyond 6 weeks.
Beta blocker e.g propranolol	Very good for exam anxiety. 'Student's friend'. Not addictive.	Not useful after 4 weeks or so. Can't be used by asthmatics at all.
Anti-epileptics e.g. pregabalin	Good long term agent	Possibly open to misuse. Can feel disorientating
Anti-psychotics e.g. haldol, olanzapine	Effective against extreme symptoms like paranoia	Too sedating for many. Weight gain side effects.

Not a comprehensive guide. For more information try a trusted website such as the NHS website (UK) .

Often, patients will get the meds from their GP or psychiatrist, and do the talking therapy with their therapist, in a 'therapeutic triangle' where each knows what is going on.

Alhamdulillah! Progress with fixing anxiety disorders is good

Anxiety disorders are treatable; success rates are far higher over the last 20 years. Talking therapies can cure things such as severe OCD, which was thought incurable for many hundreds of years. Subhanallah for the power of the spoken word, correctly delivered. Treatment is always geared to individual situations: what type of anxiety you have, how long the condition has lasted, what kinds of life situations affect you, and so on. No single plan works for everyone.

The six R's of a Strong Mind

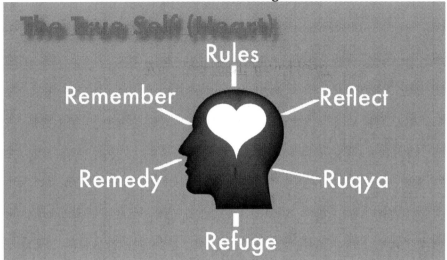

With the exception of Ruqya, these exercises can and should be used by anyone, with or without anxiety problems. They improve cognition, attention and mindfulness. Islamically, they strengthen your Heart: your true, inner self. Each of them brings tremendous benefit especially if they are done with happiness and gratitude.

Rules. These are the Rules of good Akhlaaq, and principles of good conduct. Go to my YT channel youtube.com/c/drtkharris and find the series 'building a peaceful mind. The rules of Akhlaaq are summed up there. Or look in my books Instant Insights or Instant Actions for more detailed information.

Reflection. Exercises such as kitaabat-ul-Nafs, and in fact any of the things you do in this program, are examples of reflection, as are things like du'aa and dhikr. There are many ways to contemplate the wonder of Allah, our own place in the world, and take stock of our own character.

Ruqya is a process of special du'aas and rituals that invite Allah's healing and protection for various things including illness and unseen forces. A'lims know many ways and options for specific ruqyas. I will show one example and the basic principle here, and invite you to find out more from a learned scholar or A'lim, or from a specialised source if you wish.

a) *Ruqya with blowing and placing the hand on the pain.*
 If your mind is suffering then holding the hand on your head, or blowing lightly on the head of someone who is mentally struggling.
Say Bismillah' three times, and then say seven times:
"I seek refuge with the Power and Majesty of Allah against what I suffer."

Do this as often as you like. Know that it is a gift to us as Muslims to have this method of calling on Allah to relieve pain or to live with pain more comfortably.

b)It is also permitted to recite from any Sūrah of the Quran when doing ruqya, because the whole of the Quran is a Ruqya. Allah says in the Quran:
   *"And We send down from the Quran that which is a
   healing and a mercy to those who believe."* (Al-Isrā: 82)

For issues in the mind, it is recommended to place the hand on the head, and pray any ruqya du'aa, whenever you feel like it. It takes but a few seconds to do.

Remedy. Kalonji oil or Kalonji (Black Cumin) seed is proven scientifically to have benefits on thinking, including attention, concentration and organisation. Many years before this was discovered, The prophet PBUH is said to have advised it as a cure for all things except death. Again, this is a special gift to us as Muslims. Although opinions vary on the amount, research would suggest about half a teaspoon a day, or ½ a gram of the dry product, is a promising dose.

We must also accept that alongside its scientific properties, Allah has promised us divine help through this substance, and in taking it, any small amount, will help. If we can't find it, even a sincere intention to take it, could suffice in the eyes of Allah to bring us its benefits. Allah knows best.

Remember: This is the act of remembering Allah. It is dhikr, salah, it is the process of being mindful and connected to the presence of Allah. It can be hard to concentrate on some parts of dhikr if one is struggling with concentration and mental illness, so never fear if this is the case: you can only do your best, and Allah will accept your best efforts as readily as he would the most perfect salah, because He knows when you are struggling and would not expect you to be perfect in your delivery of prayers or remembrance.

Tasbeeh (repetitions of a simple phrase) is a simple but effective method of remembrance. Keep it super simple, whatever you can manage. Saying a simple tasbeeh repeatedly can offer immense comfort and relief. Never underestimate the power of simple things.

The beads themselves provide a potent way of soothing a restless mind, keeping your count of whatever you are repeating. Alhamdulillah, Subhanallah, and Allahuakbar are the three go-to tasbeeh phrases for most of us. The process of physically counting out the tasbeeh can itself be immensely soothing to someone who is restless and jittery from anxiety. Try it if you are struggling, or offer it to someone of they are. Whatever it takes to get an inch or two forward, Allah will show you the way and reward your good intentions.

Seeking Refuge: Sanctuary and reassurance with Allah

This is a process of spiritually giving yourself completely over to Allah's mercy. It is true submission, asking His protection over you from troublesome thoughts. Through this, you could continue to have worries but your reaction to them becomes less emotionally tiring. You realise that worries do the greatest harm because we worry about them! And when we seek refuge in Allah we completely let go of that concern: we let the worries just exist, without judging them or fearing them. A Hadith about a prayer offered by the prophet when seeking protection from any illness:

أَذْهِبِ آلبَأْسَ رَبَّ النَّاسِ وَاشْفِ أَنْتَ الشَّافِي لاَ شِفَاءَ إِلاَّ شِفَاؤُكَ شِفَاءً لاَ يُغَادِرُ سَقَمًا

Adhhibi al-ba'sa rabba al-nās washfi anta al-shāfī lā shifā'a illā shifā'uk shifā'an lā yughādiru saqaman

Remove the difficulty O Lord of mankind, and heal. You are the Healer, no healing avails but Yours, a healing that leaves behind no ailment.

Such a simple and powerful du'aa.

Practicing the Six R's of a Strong Mind.

Repetition: Recommended, variable daily

All of the R's have opportunity to be done in a minor way, every day. They are better if tied in with salah times or when you have time to yourself. Go through each and lost when you might be able to do it.

Rules: Write down your Akhlaaq Rules. Glance at them and aspire to them every day.   **Do this? Yes/ No**

Reflection: variable: depends which exercise you are doing in this program.

Ruqya: Read a Ruqya du'aa once a day.   **Do this? Yes/ No**

Refuge: As part of your du'aas in salah or afterwards, read the du'aa seeking refuge, or read passages of the Quran that bring you comfort.   **Do this? Yes/ No**

Remedy: Black Cumin- daily 0.5 g of the dried seed or 1-2ml of the oil.   **Do this? Yes/ No**

Remember: Depends on the method of dhikr; Tasbeeh can be at any time, especially when restless.   **Do this? Yes/ No**

Comments/ progress notes:

How does worrying happen in the brain?

In this chapter we will:
- *Understand how the mind is composed, and where worries mainly arise from in the mind.*
- *Recognise that we have different ways to respond to our thoughts and feelings, using different parts of our mind.*

You take your car into the shop for a check-up. You think,

What if there are major problems with the engine?
Might be very expensive.
What if they don't give me a discount?
What if I might not have a car at all?
What if I can't get to work?
What if I might lose my job! I might have to borrow some money.

Spot the language. A lot of 'what ifs' and 'mights'. Seems like your mind is full of *negative possibilities, conditional events,* and jumping to conclusions.

Drilling down a bit further, we see two things happening:
1. Imagining future events
2. Considering possible solutions

If you can understand that, then you are already on the way to cracking the problem.

Here is the model of the Muslim Mind.

Deen, wisdom, and character: Heart

Emotions and Ego: Nafs   Knowledge, problem-solving: Intellect

It is in 3 parts, as you can see. Worries are rooted in the Nafs. The Nafs is typically emotional, rapid, and jumps to conclusions and exaggerations. The intellect and heart can be overpowered if they are not tuned into the Nafs.

This is what happens when we are overpowered by worries. So the good news is that worries are coming from only one of the three main sections of your brain: the other two are ready to help out. Alhamdulillah.

More than that, we can also calm the Nafs directly using things such as deep breathing. So, right from the start, we have three possible 'routes' to finding solutions. Subhanallah.

Worries typically start as what-if questions.
What if it rains? I will get wet. People will laugh. I will have to change at work. What if there's no place to do that?

Worries are thoughts about the future. Even if you're thinking about the past, your worries are about what this will mean in future. *What if my friendship with Najma is lost forever because of that argument we had? What if she tells all my secrets to other people?*

Worries are always negative. This seems obvious, but think about it this way. People don't worry that they might have a *good* time. There is no problem to solve there. The brain is a problem solving engine, so naturally, you tend to think of issues that are negative. Problems to get round. However, this can go wrong when you just see the negative side and begin imagining only negative things. You start 'catastrophising' and worst-case-scenarios feel like they might become real.

Why? The Nafs. It is primal, basic: it is designed to help you survive, but it does so by imagining scary things and keeping you away from them: this can get out of hand.

In my book Instant Insights, I explain the Nafs in great detail. Look into that book if you want to know more. It should suffice here to say that the Nafs is a part of you that has existed since birth, and we as humans have the Nafs in common with all living things. It is a potent force in keeping us safe, and sensing the world around us.

It does so by working with emotions, instincts and insecurities. It is natural to have insecurities but when they get out of hand we make poor, impulsive decisions which we often regret. And because the Nafs doesn't think in *words*, these actions can be difficult to understand afterwards because we don't have the words to understand why or how we acted.

Normal Worries versus 'Anxiety Disorders'

Aims:
- *To get a rough idea of where normal worry drifts over into disorder.*
- *To be comfortable with the idea that it is often hard to tell.*
- *To be less afraid of either state: neither is pleasant, but neither need be feared because Allah is with us. We can carry on humbly and seek solutions in either case.*

Excessive worry is defined as too much concern for a real or imagined situation, to the point where our amount of concern is harmful to us or takes on a life of its own.

For example, a chap who has lost his job and has no income can probably be **rationally worried** about getting a new job: it drives him to get up early and focus on solving the problem. It is unpleasant, but productive: he doesn't lose his sense of control on his mind, instead just keeping focussed on trying different things, or just being at peace with the concern without letting it take over.

But someone who is in a relatively stable job who worries about losing it for no sensible reason is in a state of needless, excessive, **irrational worry.**

What is needless, or what is excessive, really depends on the person, their culture and priorities, and their situation and beliefs.

There's a difference between *feelings* of panic or anxiety and anxiety *disorders*. Anyone can experience feelings of panic or anxiety, and the presence of such feelings doesn't necessarily mean you have an anxiety disorder. Only when the feelings become overwhelming and start taking over your day do they become disorders.

Things which 'kinda' work but not enough.
People try to turn away from their Nafs by keeping busy, socialising, going for a walk, cleaning, collecting things or any other action that helps keeps them distracted. However, if you're like many of the people with Generalised anxiety disorder,, these things just don't seem to work for long enough; at worst, they add to the sense that you are avoiding the worry, making things worse. That's when you know there's a problem.

Everyone worries on occasion, and this is absolutely normal. And we all tend to worry more during times of stress or major life changes.

Worry is a problem if it is present most of the day, every day, is excessive given the situation, is difficult to control, and interferes with a person's daily life or leads to significant distress.

Examples:
'I'm worried about an exam so much that I can't concentrate on studying'
'I'm so worried about a job interview that I've just cancelled it and backed out altogether. '

Life gets impaired in other ways. You might spend more time on your own, avoiding social life, or avoiding the things you used to enjoy. Your preoccupations may mean you stop taking care of other important things in your life. You lose the ability to enjoy anything because your worrying is so overpowering. This Nafs is a powerful thing if left unchecked, but it can be got back into control by careful and sensitive efforts on your part. Inshallah.

Your Mind is Your Partner

Aims of this section:
- *To clarify how Intellect and Heart can resolve worries*
- *To understand how the mind and body are connected.*

I've seen many people cry tears of joy at the relief of being freed from a mental disorder. But before this happens, so many people are trapped in unwarranted shame, avoiding help. Some are even unaware that they can be helped. May Allah help us to help them.

I believe mental disorders are often more cruel than physical ones, because they trick the person, and society at large, into believing that they are not really there, or that they are the person's own fault. May Allah give us the sense of compassion and insight to avoid this trap, Ameen.

Here is the model of the Muslim Mind again.

Your True Self: Heart

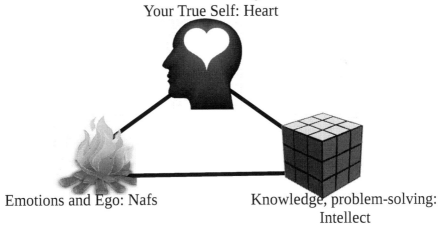

Emotions and Ego: Nafs   Knowledge, problem-solving: Intellect

Your conscious self- as you experience yourself now- is your Heart. But this part needs development and nurturance. Without it, you are a more basic creature, dominated by your Nafs, confusing immediate desires and temptations with your true wishes.

 The first point emerges: think *it's not you* who is anxious as such, nor is it even all of your brain. It is a *part of your brain, which is over-excited and dominating the scene. But noisy things can seem bigger than they really are.*

The rest of you is OK:

1. **Your Intellect** is a bit overpowered by its noisy neighbour, and is weakened by the distraction, but underneath that it is still fine. You still know that issues can be dealt with step by step.

2.**Your True self (Heart)** is able to see the bigger picture: Allah will help, and you can indeed bring out your best character if you try to remember how you would like to be. (For more guidance see my series called Akhlaaq' in Instant Insights or on youtube.)

So, you can then look at the problem from a bit of a distance, separating your more calm, rational sides from the emotional or troubled sides.

Most issues with anxiety begin with the Nafs and are felt throughout the mind and body, because the Nafs is the most basic part- we are born with it, whereas the Intellect and Heart develop later, once we are children and becoming adults respectively. The Nafs is powerful and quick, and it can overwhelm us, convincing us that our emotional reactions to things are the actual truth, when this is wrong: we only have a 'perception' of the world, which could be correct or wrong.

The Intellect tries to help but gets overwhelmed or confused. It can be listened to, if we call it forth in our calmer moments. The

Heart can help a lot but most people don't know how to use it in the way that might work.

This program is about recovering and strengthening your whole mind so that it works in sync: the Nafs is not to be demonised or suppressed. Rather, we learn to understand it and learn how to interpret and deal with it more effectively, peacefully. Fire is useful: you must learn how to use it responsibly and what to do if it does get out of control. It's no use denying it's there, and when we do control it, we would be wise to see what factors caused it so we can avoid it getting out of control in future.

Words like anxiety, stress, worry, trauma, and depression get used a lot in normal language but they mean something different in professional language. When a doctor talks to colleague saying he has a depressed patient, it is different to a person in ordinary life saying 'I'm feeling depressed'. It's therefore a confusing business s for a lay person to separate a clinical condition from the normal difficulties of life.

Stress is a condition everyone knows. Not all stress is bad; some stress is alerting and productive, alhamdulillah. You react with drive and growth. Exercise is a type of stress we induce on ourselves to cause growth. An ambitious but noble project, like building a house for homeless people, is a positive stress. It is self-perpetuating, energising us: we don't seem to mind the hard work because it has such a strong meaning. In fact, we are feeding our souls by helping others. Negative stress turns our performance downwards, draining our energy and leaving us more fearful than optimistic. May Allah help us.

Anxiety can create stress or be a response to it. Anxiety is part of the emotional response to stress. Our Nafs starts shooting out 'What if' questions which we can't answer, or the answers trouble

49

us.

Anxiety is a very real issue. The Nafs has symptoms that are:

• Emotional (dread, fearing panic, fearing social situations, etc.)
• Physical (racing heart, dizziness, shortness of breath, lump in the throat, tingling, etc.)
• Mental (worrying, preoccupation with fear, fear of dying or going crazy, etc.)

There is a difference between panic and anxiety. Many people think they "panic all day," but a true panic attack is only a few minutes at most. It is like a sudden explosion of emotion. The aftermath of a panic attack can last for hours, leaving a person tired and weak.

Short term anxiety is an intense feeling of dread, but not as filled with the dread of impending death or doom as panic is. It lasts a bit longer; more like a wave than an explosion. Anticipation of trouble. You receive a phone call saying your child is injured at school. Your father goes to the hospital with chest pain. Or your mother says, "We have to talk," with no clue of what that talk will be about. In these situations, you feel intensely worried. The nafs is connected to all the organs in the body; heart rate rises a little, you feel a bit sick, you get a bit sweaty too. Like panic disorder, the feeling of most anxiety states is as much emotional as it is physical.

Self Test: Measuring anxiety

This test will help you to understand what level of anxiety you have, and you can repeat it as you do the program to see how things are improving inshallah.

It will be immediately effective: you are now pinning the issue down with numbers and facts. Take it easy, and just do your best. Your best is always good enough for Allah, even when you don't think so. Don't spend too long on an answer: just go with your 'feeling' if you can.

1. What subjects wear you down with worry most often?

a. _____

b. _____

c. _____

d. _____

Over the last 2 weeks, have you had these issues?

Not able to stop worrying

0	1	2	3
Not at all	Some days only	A lot of the time	Nearly every day

Trouble relaxing

0	1	2	3
Not at all	Some days only	A lot of the time	Nearly every day

Feeling nervous, anxious or on edge

0	1	2	3
Not at all	Some days only	A lot of the time	Nearly every day

Being physically very restless

0	1	2	3
Not at all	Some days only	A lot of the time	Nearly every day

Irritable or snappy with other people or yourself

0	1	2	3
Not at all	Some days only	A lot of the time	Nearly every day

Feeling afraid as if something terrible might happen

0	1	2	3
Not at all	Some days only	A lot of the time	Nearly every day

Worrying too much about many different things.

0	1	2	3
Not at all	Some days only	A lot of the time	Nearly every day

What was your total score, added up? _____

Scoring formula:

Total score. Less than 5 = not significant. 6 to 10 = mild, 10 to 15 = moderate, greater than 15 = severe.

This is only a rough indication, not meant to diagnose you. However, if you are concerned about your anxiety, seek formal medical advice from your doctor. The last question is this:

How have the issues made your life? (At home, work, or socially)?

A	B	C	D
No problem	A bit hard	Very hard	Totally Impossible

If it is B, C, or D, then the program will be helpful to you inshallah, although nothing takes the pace of a live doctor so seek medical help if you are struggling. Life hurts, and life is difficult, but life should not be overwhelming, draining you of all your zest or leaving you unable to face a further moment. Seek help if this is the case.

Set a time and date in your calender to repeat this test if you like. Recommendation: weekly.

Which day of the week?   _____

What time?   _____

Note down your scores as weeks go by:

Test occasion	1	2	3	4	5	6	7	8
Score								

Tips: Again, in this program the test is not meant to diagnose you, because only a professional can do that. However, doing the test will:
a) Help you to understand the range of things that anxiety can affect
b) Give you an idea of where you are in the range of anxiety problems
c) Give you the chance to review how you are doing. Repeat the test roughly every week to get a clear idea of how things are going for you. Inshallah, you can track your improvement and spot if there are issues that you get stuck on.

Watch for feelings of depression that follow prolonged worry and anxiety. There is a big overlap between depression and generalized anxiety. You may need to see a doctor or get formal counselling if you can't cope with these things on your own. Allah demands that we look after the bodies and minds that he has lent to us.

Types of anxiety disorder

- Panic disorder
- Generalized anxiety disorder
- Panic disorder
- Social anxiety disorder
- Agoraphobia
- Specific phobia
- Post-traumatic stress disorder (PTSD)
- Obsessive-compulsive disorder (OCD)

If you fear that you are unclean after wudhu, or that germs are about to contaminate every surface you touch, your anxiety becomes **obsessive compulsive disorder (like was-was)** and you might develop habits or rituals that get out of had, repeatedly checking and cleaning.

If you get extremely anxious whenever you see a spider then you might develop a **phobia** of them: a fear of something which is in reality a tiny threat but your reaction is way overboard: irrational.

The Nafs is a specialist at reacting in an exaggerated, irrational way, because your *emotions tend to present themselves as facts.*

In reality, everyone has their own things that cause them to worry, and it may be unclear when a persistent anxiety becomes a formal 'anxiety disorder' that a doctor is called to treat.

For people who have anxiety to a clinical extent, if it's a general anxious permanent state it is called **generalised anxiety disorder** or GAD.

We will learn more about the other types of anxiety disorder as we go along.

Why see a medical family doctor if I think I might have an anxiety disorder? Surely that is all just in the mind?

Because anxiety disorders can often have a physical cause, and medical doctors understand and treat mental health issues too.

Common medical causes that can cause or mimic anxiety disorder include:
• Heart conditions
• Anaemia – low red blood cell count, caused by bleeding (low iron intake, or heavy periods etc)
• Thyroid problems
• Blood sugar imbalances (diabetes or hypoglycaemia)
• Hormone changes, including those that may accompany contraception, or disorders like thyroid conditions common in women above 30.
• Stimulating drugs, such as steroids or those prescribed for asthma, or excessive caffeine from tea and coffee.
• Medication side effects or reactions
• Breathing issues impairing oxygen intake such as obstructive airways (asthma) or sleep apnoea (in heavier people, a feeling of choking that disturbs the sleep).

It also works the other way: many people with anxiety disorders see their doctor believing there is something wrong with their heart or other organs, but the organ that is struggling is their brain. This is no less serious, but for some reason people think problems with the brain are too be ashamed of. Probably because we can't 'see' the problem or feel it in a physical sense. We're quite simple creatures really.

In its mildest form, worry is just 'concern' for something. That's not bad. It is when it grow too overwhelming for the mind, or get the mind stuck in the worry rather than focussed on solutions, that it becomes a problem or 'worry' as such.

Most of the time, *'being concerned about something'* is a basic trigger- a signal from your emotions (Nafs) to get on and prepare yourself for a situation and anticipate the outcomes. For things that are more important to you, you worry about them more. Everybody has different amounts and types of things that worry them, and we also know that Allah has designed some people genetically to be more prone to worry about stuff just by virtue of their own personality. There is benefit in having such a person in a group because they might help to make sure things are kept in order, or that the group is kept safe. Allah is all knowing and wise and made us different for a reason: we are designed to work together with each other, all having slightly different strengths and inclinations.

How Anxiety is Triggered

In this chapter we will
  • *Understand what kind of situations typically cause worries.*

Situations or events like these get the Nafs going into overdrive with worry and emotions:

1. Unpredictable
2. New events and/ or change
3. Unclear situations.

<u>Unpredictable situations</u>

We can only put in the effort into something, but we can't know the result. This is OK in life for simple things, for example tying your shoelaces. Mostly when you reach down and try to tie your shoelaces, you succeed.

But there was a time when this was not the case, right? You were a kid. The experience maybe annoyed you or worried you. That worry or that annoyance were strong emotions, and drove you to learn how to tie your shoelace properly. Psychologists call this process the *rage to master:* a strong emotionally driven mechanism. In this way, the energy from their Nafs can put the Intellect (the problem solving part of the brain) into action by motivating it to learn something.

Exams are less predictable than tying your shoelaces. You can prepare all you like but the results of the exam are not within your control.

What if the questions are unclear? What is I miss a page? What if I am anxious when I take the exam? Did I study the right

57

material? What if I forget what I revised?

There's no way to predict exactly what will be on the exam. You try to compensate, by studying all you can, but it's not enough. You forget some stuff and suddenly your Nafs convinces you that you will forget everything! You get a mental block and you start panicking. You breathe rapidly and you sweat: now your whole body is involved in the act, making you feel even worse. Fear and anxiety have the strange effect of feeding on themselves, getting bigger each time. This is designed to help you escape a threat, but when you need to be calm, it can make things difficult. Your performance ends up reflecting your anxiety rather than your true ability.

New situations

I've been called to a work colleague's house for food. Do they know I only eat halal meat? Would it be rude to ask them not to drink alcohol when I am there? What if I simply don't like the food? What if they have pets like dogs?

Your Nafs loves running away with itself, and will trick your intellect into solving endless scary problems if you let it.

Maybe I could tell them. How would they react? And what if they forget? Maybe I should not go at all.

Uncertainty is part of everyone's life. It is a mixed thing: it often brings growth and development. Allah encourages us to seek new things and growth; we are even told to accept wisdom from the mouth of a *mushrik* (one who has committed the grave sin of ascribing partners to God) if that wisdom itself is true.

Unclear situations

Someone has asked to visit me at home. I don't know them very well. What if they hurt me or steal from me? What if they are going to tell me some terrible news?

When you simply don't have the facts to hand, a lack of clarity justifies some caution. It could quite possibly be a very positive outcome; maybe this person wanted to make you a fantastic job offer, or wanted to ask you to help them with a wonderful project

But those are not problems. Nobody worries about good things happening. Your Nafs looks for issues which are problems, and inserts its own imagined problems into the situation. It had good intentions: to prepare you for unexpected bad things- but this backfires because your anticipation and reaction itself is harmful and excessive: worry makes you overcautious and terrified, and you might miss out on a good opportunity.

The physical side of worry

Aims:

- *Understand how the Nafs is very physically connected to the rest of our body*
- *Recognise that the Nafs can make the body tense, and vice versa.*
- *Recognise the harms that come from worrying intensely over a long time.*

Physically, the functions of the Nafs are mostly located in the inner and lower parts of the brain, where emotions and instincts are found and a lot of the information from our nerves and senses is processed.

It is connected with the body through the nervous system and various hormones and other messengers. When you are anxious, your body feels it in all the organs. Your heart rate goes up, your breathing gets more rapid, your skin sweats, your muscles twitch, and so on. This makes a lot of sense. The Nafs is helping you to survive, so these changes are all designed to put you into a state where you can overcome a threat: the infamous 'flight or fight' thing.

I've borrowed a page from Instant Insights to show you here next.

When our emotions run high, we can notice the following things:

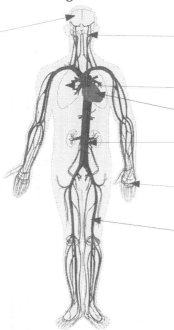

Reduced blood flow to logical and rational areas: mind goes blank.

Increased blood flow to emotional areas: Anxiety, anger, arousal

Breathing rate higher
Heart rate higher

Butterflies in the stomach

Sweating

More blood flow to muscles: they are readier to go into action.

- Blood flow to the emotional regions increases, making emotions get stronger.
- Blood flow to the upper areas of the brain- where logic and language reside- is actually decreased, making us lose the capacity to think things through properly, and feel 'lost for words'.
- Heart rate and breathing rate go up. We feel our heart pumping, and our breathing gets shallow and rapid.
- Blood flow to the gut decreases, giving us a feeling of butterflies.
- Bloodflow to the muscles increases, giving us the feeling of nervous energy, ready to run or fight.

Physical signs in someone who is permanently or excessively anxious can become harmful over time. This is how:

1. First of all, it's mentally exhausting. Mood and morale drop.
2. It's distracting: you can't keep your mind of the tasks in front of you. Driving and other issues can become difficult and tiring.
3. It can worsen to become a state of despair or depression.
4. Your skin suffers from excess sweat and oil secretion: spots, rashes, and hair loss. Hair can become grey prematurely.
5. Stomach acids increase in stress, leading to heartburn and ulcers.
6. Your gut becomes irritated and issues like irritable bowel syndrome, intermittent diarrhoea and constipation crop up.
7. Your kidneys get stressed out and you need to urinate more often.
8. The body can't manage its hormones properly and issues like weight gain, troublesome appetite and diabetes can happen.
9. The heart gets stressed out from beating fast all the time, and your blood pressure goes up. Rick of heart attack and strokes (blood clots in the brain) go up.

Now what was the point of this big long list? Surely I am not trying to scare you. Of course not. The point is to illustrate just how much of an influence the Nafs has on your body.

Anxiety: your body's alarm system

A good way to think of the Nafs is like an alarm system. Alarms tell you when something's in danger. They alert you. But if they're constantly going off then you can't get much done, and you get exhausted and worn out. False alarms are very tiresome.

In Instant Insights we talk in more detail about how the Nafs is geared to protect us. In summary, it is a strong force but it is

Get Videos & Books, Raise Funds drtkharris.wordpress.com

rather blunt and unsophisticated: it's a bit like fire in that way. It can be useful or harmful, depending on how we understand it and deal with it.

Although anxiety is great for moving you into action when physical danger is present, it's not so good when the threat is social. It gets in the way, making you fear things that probably won't happen. But it is the only system we have, designed with great wisdom by Allah. I believe that social shyness is helpful and protective to a degree: if everybody was fully socially competent we would not have the wondrous things that come about from a shy and sensitive heart, or from a person who works alone making or writing about great things. Everything has a purpose, even if the person who has it doesn't find it pleasant.

Allah has provided us with Akl (intellect) and Qalb (Heart) to manage the Nafs and to give us many alternate ways of getting ahead in the world. Ideally, we would spend more of our time listening to and nurturing those parts. Which is partly what this book will help you to do.

Worry symptoms under the microscope

Worry about everyday things
Family, work or school, finances, their health and the health of loved ones, relationships with friends or colleagues, punctuality, and making small decisions.Everybody has these kinds of worries but if the worrying takes over your life to the point where you can't deal with these issues properly, you have a problem. Alhamdulillah. Let us investigate.

You've probably found that your worries are always in the background. Some days you might worry more and some days you might worry less, but there isn't much time when you are worry-free. It's like the Nafs is now an anxious torchlight, and everything that comes under your attention becomes a source of worry.

Not sleeping well
It's very common for worriers. The minute you put your head to the pillow, worries start spinning in your head. your mind is free to start worrying. You actually worry less during the day when you're busy, distracted by other things.

Some people fall asleep OK but can't remain asleep. They wake up several times a night, awoken by their worries. Even when you sleep, your mind is still working, and whatever you worried about that day can carry over into the night. Nightmares are a problem too. The Nafs is especially strong at night when the Intellect and Conscious mind are not awake. Inhibitions are freed up even more and night time can seem a scary place.

Being a worrier means you are like every other human being except you have to do things with a big fire behind you, always causing you to rush, get frightened, or get exhausted. This is mentally and physically exhausting.

Can't concentrate

 If you're busy paying attention to worries then you cant focus on something that's in front of you.

You wander through the world hardly noticing much of it because your Nafs is living in another time, either in the past or future, and you don't have time for the present moment. You might steal a moment or two to remember this or that little detail, but your memory seems poor because you simply aren't laying down much new stuff in your brain for today: you are focussed on other times.

Feeling restless, edgy jittery

The natural consequence of having a Nafs which is primed for threat means that you are always alert to something going wrong. Your pupils are dilated, your heart races, your muscles are twitchy and jittery, your mind is jumpy. Adrenaline is soaking your tissues through and through, so to speak.

These things may not be noticed by others, or even yourself. The brain has a curious way of adapting to things. Many people with long term anxiety have no idea that this is a different state of mind; it becomes their 'new normal'. Even other people don't notice it in them. I suppose it's a little like the duck's feet: on the surface the duck looks calm but underneath its feet are paddling rapidly.

Being Snappy or Easily Annoyed

Anxiety is like a fog in that it spreads throughout the brain with soft edges. Just because you are worried about A all the time it doesn't mean you wont worry about B; in fact, the 'attitude' or being worried sort of infects the other things in your mind, so

65

even a benign question or interruption from someone else comes across as threatening or rude to you momentarily, and you react angrily. You might realise instantly what you've done, but sometimes you might not. It can really get in the way of your relationships with people.

Having worries to this disabling extent doesn't necessarily mean you will become a pessimistic person; in fact, many people with anxiety issues know that in their day to day lives they are very optimistic, and losing this optimism is a sign that their anxiety issues have returned.

Muscle tension and twitches

Anxiety causes blood to be diverted out of your gut and toward your muscles, priming them for action. This heightened state puts them on edge, ready to fire, like a sprung coil. Being in this state for long periods makes them tighten up, misfire and ache. This is particularly noticeable in the smaller muscles in the neck and in the muscles that take care of posture in your back.

Generalised anxiety is worry constantly about a wide variety of things. The Nafs is in a general state of overload. It is as if anything you think about is painted with a worry brush.

It really limits life. The gnawing feeling in the gut, the preoccupation and loss of attention, the sense of doom and misery, and the physical agitation all combine to create major problems and suffering participating in life. Loss of pleasure, constant worry, poor sleep. Life becomes a drag.

Self test: Detailed anxiety scoring.

This test is for those who already know they have anxiety diagnosed as a clinical problem. Skip this part if it doesn't apply to you. Rate your symptoms over the last 2 weeks.

1. Anxious Mood
Worries, fearing the worst, irritability.

0	1	2	3	4
None	Mild	Moderate	Severe	Extreme

2. Tension
Easily tired, easily crying, exhausted, feeling stressed out.

0	1	2	3	4
None	Mild	Moderate	Severe	Extreme

3. Fears
Strangers, being alone, crowds, animals.

0	1	2	3	4
None	Mild	Moderate	Severe	Extreme

4. Insomnia
Difficulty in sleep, staying asleep, nightmares,

0	1	2	3	4
None	Mild	Moderate	Severe	Extreme

5. Thinking is difficult. Poor focus, distractability.

0	1	2	3	4
None	Mild	Moderate	Severe	Extreme

6. Low Mood
Loss of interest, lack of pleasure, depression, early morning waking, mood improves with the day.

0	1	2	3	4
None	Mild	Moderate	Severe	Extreme

7. Muscular

Aches and pains, stiffness, twitching, grinding of teeth, unsteady voice

0	1	2	3	4
None	Mild	Moderate	Severe	Extreme

8. Sensory

Ringing ears, blurred vision, hot and cold flushes, weakness, tingling

0	1	2	3	4
None	Mild	Moderate	Severe	Extreme

9. Heart Symptoms

Heart racing, pain in central chest, throbbing

0	1	2	3	4
None	Mild	Moderate	Severe	Extreme

10. Breathing Symptoms

Pressure or constriction in chest, choking feelings, sighing, difficulty breathing

0	1	2	3	4
None	Mild	Moderate	Severe	Extreme

11. Gut Symptoms

Difficulty in swallowing, wind, indigestion, pain before and after meals, burning sensations, uncomfortable bloating, nausea, vomiting, sinking feelings, diarrhoea or constipation, weight changes.

0	1	2	3	4
None	Mild	Moderate	Severe	Extreme

12. Urinary
Urinating a lot or more often, loss of periods, heavy periods, premature ejaculation, loss of erection, uncomfortable sexual disturbance

0	1	2	3	4
None	Mild	Moderate	Severe	Extreme

13. Nerve Symptoms
Dry mouth, flushing of the cheeks, paleness, sweatiness, giddiness, tension

0	1	2	3	4
None	Mild	Moderate	Severe	Extreme

Scoring Totals::
0-12: No significant issue.
13-24 Mild problem
25-36 A significant problem
36-48 Very distressing problem

This test, like many of the tests in this program, is derived from a valid research tool which has been tested, refined, revised and retested and found to be accurate across many thousands of people.

Set a time and date in your calender to repeat this test if you like:

Recommendation: weekly.Which day of the week? _____

What time?_____

Note down your scores as weeks go by:

Test occasion	1	2	3	4	5	6	7	8
Score								

All about Panic disorder

Panic attacks are bouts of sudden, intense feelings (physical sensations and emotions) of fear or terror that last up to 15 minutes. They typically leave you feeling weak, exhausted, and scared for minutes or even hours after the attack subsides.

Your body has an effective alarm system which relies on a sudden burst of adrenaline when you face a severe threat all of a sudden. This is meant to happen when we face a very sudden threat, such as for example if you saw a lion or slipped down a cliff. The Nafs wakes up quickly, believing that you are facing immediate threat of severe injury or death. Images of these things flash across your mind, and blood is sent to your muscles, making your heart race, and giving you a feeling of butterflies in the stomach and itchiness all of a sudden. If the situation is real, your nafs could well save your life.

We can think of panic *disorder* as when the brain's alarm system is set off in the wrong situation. You might be a little afraid of something, such as doing something silly, but your Nafs takes over and sees it as a dire threat. You end up believing the Nafs because it is very quick and emotional.

If the situation is not actually threatening, you still believe there is a threat anyway: adrenaline will do that. Your Nafs goes into overdrive, logic goes out of the window because blood supply to your intellect is cut down too, and you react on instinct and fear. This is very unpleasant and embarrassing, and feeds itself.

<u>Fear of public spaces, or agoraphobia</u>

It sometimes develops as a result of avoiding panic attacks. Your Nafs has a drive for security and safety, avoiding negative consequences at all costs. The avoidance offers so much relief

Get Videos & Books, Raise Funds drtkharris.wordpress.com

that the subsequent loss of social life doesn't matter to the Nafs: it is interested only in keeping you safe, and would hide you from all threats if it could, small or big.

Some people rarely leave their homes, whereas others go out but only to a few places and with people they know. Inability to escape is a key concern. Remember, the Nafs is primal and focussed on safety: it wishes to know its escape routes if threatened.

Self Test: Do I Have Panic Disorder?

If you have experienced at least one panic attack, which of the following things have happened? Tick the appropriate number:

1. I have worried about having panic attacks so much that it has got in the way of home, work or social life.

0	1	2	3
Not at all	*A little bit*	*A fair amount*	*Very much so*

2. I have stopped attending activities you previously enjoyed.

0	1	2	3
Not at all	*A little bit*	*A fair amount*	*Very much so*

3. I have limited travelling to places or paths where I feel safe from panic

0	1	2	3
Not at all	*A little bit*	*A fair amount*	*Very much so*

4. I avoided transportation that you think you might panic on such as buses, trains, etc.

0	1	2	3
Not at all	*A little bit*	*A fair amount*	*Very much so*

5. I have avoided social situations where I might panic (e.g. jamaat salah, gatherings of people)

0	1	2	3
Not at all	*A little bit*	*A fair amount*	*Very much so*

6. I have started paying attention to exits and ways to escape a location

0	1	2	3
Not at all	*A little bit*	*A fair amount*	*Very much so*

7. I have seen a doctor or searched online to make sure I was not having a heart attack.

0	1	2	3
Not at all	*A little bit*	*A fair amount*	*Very much so*

8. I have stayed home from school or work for fear of having an attack

0	1	2	3
Not at all	*A little bit*	*A fair amount*	*Very much so*

9. I have stopped praying where I might be seen, or shopping in stores where people might see me panicking

0	1	2	3
Not at all	*A little bit*	*A fair amount*	*Very much so*

10. I asked someone to be with me when travelling even for short distances,

0	1	2	3
Not at all	*A little bit*	*A fair amount*	*Very much so*

Add up your total score: _____

0-10 = You don't have panic disorder. Occasional issue might crop up; do keep an eye on it if things worsen. You can control panic better than you can control situations or people.

11-20 = You are starting to change your behaviour to accommodate panic. Ask yourself if giving up activities or making life more complicated is really better than managing panic.

21-30= Signs of clinical level panic disorder. Carry on with the work, and seek help if you find that it feels uncontrollable. You are certainly afraid of feeling afraid!

31-40 or more = It's controlling your life. You can continue here but don't wait too long before seeking help if you can.

Set a time and date in your calender to repeat this test if you like:

Recommendation: weekly.

Which day of the week?   _____

What time?   _____

Note down your scores as weeks go by:

Test occasion	1	2	3	4	5	6	7	8
Score								

 The problem with avoiding situations which cause panic attacks is that it shuts your options of life down. Your life becomes restricted and isolated. This just feeds into itself and your mental health takes a beating as a result. You give up your control and hand it over to the panic.

We define a Panic Attack as a feeling of fear that begins suddenly and builds rapidly in intensity, usually reaching a peak in less than 10 minutes. Also there are is racing or pounding heart, shortness of breath, choking, dizziness, sweating, trembling. There are also distressing thoughts like fear of death or losing control.

Social anxiety

Allah makes us all different. Part of the joy of being you is being your individual self. You should try to be your best self, not someone else. Their job is already taken! There is nothing wrong as such with being shy, and most shy people have satisfying lives. Shyness is positive if you think that shy people are often more thoughtful, they notice things others don't, and they are often very creative and imaginative because of time spent on their own: ironically enough, shy people often hold on to Allah more closely because they rarely feel shy on front of Him.

But when you have social anxiety, you avoid experiences that could help you grow and develop your abilities. Social anxiety may be something you have a genetic tendency towards. It can be seen in childhood, adolescence, or adulthood. Most people with social anxiety experience their anxiety as too uncomfortable to tolerate. They are sensitive to the very feeling of anxiety and try to avoid feeling it.

There are three categories of common symptoms for social anxiety:
a) uncomfortable being observed, b) being judged for social mistakes, and c) not knowing how to 'be'.

Is Social Anxiety Interfering With Your Life?
Your social anxieties are interfering with your life if you avoid any of the following:
Going into new situations
Going to important deen gatherings such as jamaat prayers
Auditioning or interviewing for work.
Speaking up in meetings or classes.
Talking to other people at work or socially.

Self-test: Do I have social anxiety?

SECTION A: FEARS
Do you fear being observed while:
1.Eating where other people can see you?

0	1	2	3
Not at all	*A little bit*	*A fair amount*	*Very much so*

2. Signing or writing things in front of others?

0	1	2	3
Not at all	*A little bit*	*A fair amount*	*Very much so*

3. Answering a question in a group

0	1	2	3
Not at all	*A little bit*	*A fair amount*	*Very much so*

4. Speaking up at a meeting

0	1	2	3
Not at all	*A little bit*	*A fair amount*	*Very much so*

5. Leaving your place during jamaat salah or some other seated situation.

0	1	2	3
Not at all	*A little bit*	*A fair amount*	*Very much so*

SECTION B: JUDGMENTS
Do you fear that in social situations you will:
6. Not be able to think of interesting things to say

0	1	2	3
Not at all	*A little bit*	*A fair amount*	*Very much so*

7. Not be likeable

0	1	2	3
Not at all	*A little bit*	*A fair amount*	*Very much so*

8. Blush or be silent when meeting new people

0	1	2	3
Not at all	*A little bit*	*A fair amount*	*Very much so*

9. Reveal some social inadequacy, such as wearing the wrong clothes, or not know manners.

0	1	2	3
Not at all	*A little bit*	*A fair amount*	*Very much so*

10. Embarrass yourself by saying the wrong thing

0	1	2	3
Not at all	*A little bit*	*A fair amount*	*Very much so*

SECTION C: ASSUMPTIONS
Do you:
11. Assume others know the right way to do things?

0	1	2	3
Not at all	*A little bit*	*A fair amount*	*Very much so*

12. Assume you are the only one who doesn't know the right answers or who has ever made a mistake learning something new?

0	1	2	3
Not at all	*A little bit*	*A fair amount*	*Very much so*

13. Believe that you will be rejected in new situations

0	1	2	3
Not at all	*A little bit*	*A fair amount*	*Very much so*

14. Assume that other people are watching you when you are in public

0	1	2	3
Not at all	*A little bit*	*A fair amount*	*Very much so*

15. Believe that feeling humiliated is inevitable and you won't be able to get over it?

0	1	2	3
Not at all	A little bit	A fair amount	Very much so

Now add up your score. What is the total? _____
Scoring:
0-15: You do not have social anxiety disorder. Everyone feels these things from time to time.

16-30 = Mild to moderate problem. You could do with some help. You can work with the program inshallah.

31-40: It's a big and distressing problem. The program will help on its own, but do seek medical or therapy help if you feel overwhelmed.
Set a time and date in your calendar to repeat this test if you like:

Recommendation: weekly.

Which day of the week?   _____

What time?   _____

Note down your scores as weeks go by:

Test occasion	1	2	3	4	5	6	7	8
Score								

Performance anxiety

Performance anxiety is a form of social anxiety. It's when you have one specific social situation that gives you anxiety—such as leading jamaat prayer, praying alongside others, talking or being seen in public, or standing up in a classroom.

The Nafs, in wishing to keep you secure, is also concerned with how other people see you or judge you. This concern can get turned up too high, interfering with how you just do simple things that you would be able to do fine on your own. Everybody has this to an extent. The emotions take over the mind, overpowering your intellect, impairing your ability to do things calmly, and your performance may well suffer, which fulfils your fear and so the cycle gets worse.

Some people's performance can improve in public: they thrive on being observed and measured, and indeed, we see that the brain secretes hormones that can heighten enjoyment of a task if we are confident of being observed. Interestingly, these same people can flip over to the opposite too, and be crippled by the chance of being observed.

It may be intense enough to make you avoid that situation at all costs, but it is restricted to that one situation. There are many treatments, including things you can do yourself, that can cure the performance anxiety. We will be looking at these as part of the general techniques to manage anxiety in this program. There are also professional methods such as therapists who use CBT, and neurological techniques such as EMDR. Alhamdulillah, as mentioned in the beginning, we have many routes to treating these conditions that are so much better than even 20 years ago.

Phobias
A fear of a specific thing, such as snakes, spiders, or insects.

Alhamdulillah, the Nafs in all living creatures is there since birth, sometimes with very specific fears programmed in. Even a newborn baby, that has never seen an animal, will show a 'startle response' if shown a picture of an animal with sharp teeth. Alhamdulillah: these safety mechanisms have protected us and other animals from dangerous situations. And so with phobias, there is usually some kind of primal fear which then gets out of hand. For example, fearing spiders is out of a natural fear of being bitten or poisoned. Fear of heights is from a natural fear of being in a risky position of falling and being hurt.

  Many people suffer from phobias, which usually cause only minor interference with life. Some specific phobias—like fear of the dark, driving over a bridge, or claustrophobia—interfere with many life situations and therefore need attention.

Phobias can usually be treated fairly easily with any of several 'desensitization' methods, sometimes called 'ERP' or Exposure and response prevention. An example would be with a spider phobia, the person is shown a picture of a spider and spends time looking at it, then sees a moving video of one, then perhaps a dead one in a glass box, etc. You get the idea: slowly approaching the real thing. When the phobia is the outcome of a traumatic experience, the right treatment depends on the type of event and the kinds of repercussions still present in your life.

Post Traumatic Stress Disorder (PTSD)

PTSD is a serious condition may affect you as the result of any experience:
• That threatened your life or the life of someone else in your presence
• That created a sense of terror and impending emotional or physical injury
• In which you were not in control, such as a natural disaster, war, or crime

Life can and does hurt people without warning and without them apparently deserving it. Children get hurt by parents or strangers, people have terrible accidents or diseases that were not their fault, and disasters happen. People can get shocked beyond comprehension.

Their mind is unable to 'file away' the memory, and it keeps getting replayed. They walk around with a deep, unshakeable sense of dread, guilt, flashbacks, and anxiety. They can become confused, sad or angry too, and the emotions don't settle down over time as they would normally. This is the beginnings of post traumatic stress.

They may begin to experience serious symptoms that disrupt their lives and wellbeing. Nightmares, flashbacks in which they re-experience all or part of the trauma, and triggers which they avoid. Issues such as questioning their Deen, disillusionment with Allah, and thoughts of suicide also occur. Many people feel guilty for surviving the trauma and lose their sense of purpose to life.

They may become depressed or anxious, have trouble concentrating or sleeping, and become easily agitated or even angry and full of rage. These symptoms usually appear about 4 to

81

12 weeks after the event, but sometimes they don't occur for many months or even years. Some people's personality gets bound up in the trauma: this is sometimes called Complex PTSD.

Deen can help. Terrible things can happen, and we may not ever know why, at least in this world. We cannot know Allah's intentions or motives. We only know this: Allah wishes all things for the better, and just because we cannot see the benefit, it does not mean that Allah has abandoned us. All we are guaranteed is that Allah will dispense justice and comfort in the end.

Not everyone gets PTSD as a result of trauma. It depends on your vulnerability at the time. Age, personality, supportive home situation, and other factors play a role.

Firefighters, emergency room workers, and relief workers have training, so they may not have the stress response to the traumatic event that an amateur might, but even they may develop PTSD if they don't manage their inevitable mental stresses from being exposed to those situations repeatedly.

Several types of special treatment have been found to be very effective, including EMDR, rapid resolution therapy (RRT), brainspotting, energy "tapping" by various names, and many other useful approaches. If you suffer from PTSD or suspect that you do, consult a doctor (GP or psychiatrist) or a clinical psychologist. Although PTSD is broadly categorised in anxiety disorders, I will cover PTSD in another program because it is a special area which has warrants its own attention. However, don't stop reading: people with PTSD have far higher rates of anxiety disorders, and so this program will very likely be of use to you if you so wish. Help is available!

Obsessive Compulsive disorder or OCD
(aka *was-was* in some forms)

Obsessive-compulsive disorder (OCD) is one of the more 'biological' conditions in that it may or may not be caused by a life event. It often has a strong genetic cause. You can be taught to worry too much or be too cautious, but you can't be taught to be a compulsive hand-washer, checker, or hoarder. It seems to emerge in certain types of people, typically those with a high degree of conscientiousness.

OCD affects some people right at the heart of their sense of wellbeing: their deen. In this case it is often called *was-was*, a term which refers to it being 'whisperings' from Shaytan, who convinced the Nafs that something terrible will happen or is about to happen, and to do things to prevent the bad event. The thoughts are called the **obsessions**.

The responses to the thoughts- the habits or rituals that people develop- are called the **compulsions**. They include physical habits such as repeated checking, or cleaning, or special ways of arranging things, or mental habits such as repeated chants or prayers offered out of fear, or counting.

Feeling that wudhu or salah is not accepted, repeating these things time and time again out of fear- these can be particularly cruel, and Allah invites us to seek refuge in Him from these things.

Why it emerges at a certain age is not well understood, but some OCD may be triggered by infections and other events in life such as losing a loved one.

Signs of OCD include unreasonable, repeated worries and fears.

Some compulsions, like repeated hand-washing, are obvious, but others are much more subtle, such as touching a 'lucky item' or walking in a very specific way, or repeatedly returning to the same spot to make sure something is done in an Islamic way, such as leaving the house with the right foot with the right du'aa, and needing to do this 10 times for example.

The techniques in this program that involve calming your Nafs that will help you if you have OCD, but the cognitive techniques for general anxiety disorder are not well suited to OCD because they make the person focus even more on the troubling thoughts. Specific help, often professional help, is more useful, and should be sought because it can cure the condition. Do not try general anxiety management techniques like CBT for anxiety if you have OCD: the problem may well get worse because your mind just becomes more preoccupied with ideas of 'precision' and paying attention to the symptoms- the very problem.

Conditions associated with anxiety

Some common mental health conditions can cause anxiety or intensify anxiety, and they confuse the picture as to whether a discrete anxiety disorder exists. Three in particular should be mentioned: attention-deficit disorder (ADD/HD), autism spectrum disorder (ASD); and addiction.

ADHD and autism are called 'executive disorders'. The 'fault' is not within the Nafs, Intellect or Heart, but in the connections between these three part of the mind. It is as if the person has the wisdom and the intellect but can't make the ready connections between the parts of the brain, so they end up being stuck without knowing what to do, or over-focussing on just one thing.

Attention-Deficit Hyperactivity Disorder (ADD/HD)

1 in 20 people has it. So many people who have it don't know they have it; just as many people who don't have it believe they do have it. Ut is one of the harder assessments to undertake by a clinician, typically taking around three hours for a basic evaluation. This is because the symptoms are not 'specific' to ADD/HD, but are cumulative: that is, it's the amount of combined issues that add up to tell you that it is present. The person has inattention, hyperactivity, or impulsivity, alone or in combination, to the extent that these issues dominate their life and they have no idea how to stop them, despite their best effort.

Allah makes people different for reasons that are not obvious to us, but it is quite possible that the 'tendency to ADD/HD' exists as part of the rich variety of types of people there are. People with the disorder are often good at certain things other people are not good at. Typically, these things include being good at acting in emergencies, or being good at athletics, or being very innovative

85

and creative. Many different and unusual types of giftedness can occur: it depends on the person. However, even those people can suffer because of their condition and they deserve help of they ask for it.

The issue is highly genetic- almost as genetic as your physical height. And the person doesn't respond to advice. They know what to do: it's just that they can't do what they know.

They feel anxious about the way their problems with attention interfere with remembering, following through, and completing work assignments or schoolwork.

ADD/HD may go unrecognized for a long time, especially if hyperactivity isn't there. They develop anxiety as a sort of 'partly helpful' response: worrying about things gives them the ability to focus on things that they often get wrong, hopefully correcting the problem. But this is exhausting and unreliable. Life becomes a confusing, overwhelming experience.

Because they often have trouble organizing, finding workable methods to help track responsibilities is a challenge. They are prone to tiresome accidents, such as spilling, breaking, or losing things.

The best remedy for anxiety about the real problems created by ADD/HD is actively treating the disorder with strategies and medication when appropriate.

Do You Have ADD/ ADHD?

The *ASRS v1.1 screener,* easily found online by just typing those words in, gives you an idea whether you *might* have the condition. If you screen positive and you believe the problem is interfering with your life, then do seek help from your GP at first. For children, it is better to take the child directly to a paediatrician or child psychiatrist.

Autism Spectrum Conditions

About 1 in 100 people has autism, but many others, particularly men, are 'on the spectrum', having features of it but not the full disorders as such.

Again, Allah has given us different gifts and burdens. There is seldom a burden without a benefit alongside it. Sometimes this is clearly seen in people with autism, in their special abilities with paying attention to detail for example. Autistic people and those with ADHD or other conditions such as dyslexia are not 'illnesses' requiring 'cure' but they are more like 'lifelong conditions' which sometimes need help because the person wants to get along in society where most people don't have the condition.

I would be careful about creating stereotypes: many people with executive disorders have many different abilities and burdens, and it is up to them and the people around them to help these things shine. We must as a society encourage people to show their strengths more; too often we become preoccupied with what folk can't do, forgetting what they can do, sometimes better than most other people!

Symptoms of autism may include:
• Sensitivity to environmental stimulation
• Social awkwardness and lack of responsiveness to emotional signals from others
• Body language or tone of speech that is mismatched to the social situation.

• Indirect or very brief eye contact
• Intense, narrow interests
• Seen by peers as "odd", often 'shy' or 'geeky' but often 'genius at certain things such as computers or specialist knowledge areas.

In new situations people with ASD may feel intense anxiety; thus, they make efforts to avoid new and unfamiliar circumstances. They like things just so, and can appear cold and insensitive to others because they don't pick up on body language. This is often not true on the inside: they are often very sensitive indeed and become very distressed by how they might miss how other people feel, or that they come across cold. When in reality they are very soft and warm but don't know how to show it or even access it. May Allah help us all.

Addictions

This program will help you a lot with anxiety issues that underpin many addictions. Anxiety was there before the addiction came, leading the person to the addiction itself. Other people develop anxiety conditions alongside or after their addictions, as a direct result of the problem or some of the social and medical consequences of addiction. May Allah help us all to realise that why addictions may have originated in a poor choice made at one stage, their continuation is not something which we ought to blame the person for.

The Nafs is extremely sensitive to repeated behaviours and habits: if you think about it, having a fixed routine of doing the same thing is about the safest thing that a person can do. and addictions are basically feeding a powerful emotional need, sometimes at a physical level. If I showed you brains scans of people with various addictions, I could show you clear differences between those brains and non-addicted ones: a chemical deficit is definitely present, and then leads the person to do things that they really don't want to do but, with great shame and self-loathing, they nonetheless feel compelled to do. People deserve sympathy and love, and although even an addict is responsible for his or her behaviour in the end, we need not add bad judgment or social stigma to someone who is already struggling.

Many people with anxiety turn to addictions to distract or calm themselves. Addictions, whether behavioural or to a substance such as drugs and alcohol, are harmful in themselves, costing physical or great financial or social consequences. And removing the addiction is just the beginning: if the underlying reason for the addiction- the cause of the anxiety- isn't addressed, then the chance of relapse is high. Unfortunately relapse rates for many addictions are still above 90%, which is probably why Allah has cautioned against using substances. They offer some short term relief from anxiety, having some short term benefit perhaps. That's why people use them! But overall they do much more harm than good. Society is surely not confused about this, even if alcohol or drugs are permitted legally.

Addiction treatment programs or 12-step self- help programs can be very helpful in keeping a person free from the addiction: organisations ending in 'Anonymous' such as Alcoholics anonymous, Gamblers Anonymous and so on. Muslims sometimes get put off these because of the taboo of being thought of as addicted to something haraam, but also because the philosophy of their '12-step' program can seem slightly religiously inclined towards a 'Christian' model, often involving prayers to God.

This is a shame and a mistake: there is only one God after all, and praying to him as a Muslim is valid even if there are non-Muslims

89

around you doing the same thing. If you think an 'anonymous' group might help, go along! There is usually one in your area in most countries; check online.

Here are some bullet points:
• Stimulant abuse (coffee, cigarettes, cocaine) can trigger anxiety that persists into recovery.
• You may develop addiction if you use alcohol, food, or the Internet to handle anxiety or social fears.
• Alcohol causes a rebound to more intense anxiety.
• Addiction may both calm anxiety and cause it as financial, interpersonal, health, and legal issues surrounding addiction begin to mount.

More than ever, the single most powerful factor in preventing relapse is to remove access to the temptation altogether. To avoid anywhere it is near you, and to dismiss it from your home and life.

This is easier said than done for some things, such as internet based gambling and porn, but still, there are apps and other methods that can help put some barriers up. Let's remember that only a few years ago we just had phones to phone people. Some addicts have found a great deal of peace by getting rid of their ironically named 'smartphone' and getting an old Nokia instead.
If you suffer with addiction and want direct help, do see a specialist. I will be covering addictions in a future interactive program too inshallah.

Reassurance Technique: The theory

Aim: To understand and practice firm self belief, and belief in Allah, to defuse anxiety.

People with mental health problems often ask me what they can do to feel more contained by Allah's protection. In answering this question, I have considered what it means to feel protected. There are a couple of things that will help.

1. Repetition. Memorising the du'aa and just saying out loud or under your breath, several times a day, will help.

2. Seeking reassurance that works. People who seek reassurance from others, or from the Internet, ask the question 'Can you or the Internet give me the belief that I will be OK?' It is easy to see why this backfires. Belief is something that comes from within you, granted by Allah and nurtured by yourself. The reassurance you really seek is as follows. Ask yourself:

> *'How can I believe in myself and Allah so that I can handle the problem?'*

The solution then becomes more clear. To solve an emotional problem, you have two parts of your mind that can help:

- a) The Intellect: Like a scientist. Seeking truth and facts, and using calm logic.

- b) The Heart: Like the Captain of a ship. Using self belief, and faith in Allah, to rise above everything with an attitude of steadiness and perspective that sees through a storm.

These parts of the mind are not used enough when we are emotionally preoccupied. So we need to work out what our Intellect and Heart could do to get back in to the game. Here are some ideas:

1. State simple facts and evidence of when things have worked out.

'I have got through problems before, by focussing on solutions. Paying attention to solutions and trying different things out is the way forward.'

2. State higher wisdoms.

'There is nothing that happens without Allah's knowledge or will. If he wills me to get better, he can do so in an instant. If I am to remain troubled, the effect is that I am being drawn closer to Allah. If that is the case, Subhanallah. He will remove troubles when it is the perfect time to do so. I will keep trying whatever I can, safe in this knowledge'.

Exercise: Reassurance in any type of worry.

Say Bismillah. Then say

'Remove the difficulty O Lord of mankind, and heal. You are the Healer, no healing avails but Yours, a healing that leaves behind no ailment.'

Now, name your worry or worries. Just brief headlines or words.

_____

_____

Next, fill out these answers

- Allah can fix my worry if He wishes to:

1	2	3	4	5

Strongly disagree   *Strongly Agree*

- With this program, I am making humble but honest efforts to help myself:

1	2	3	4	5

Strongly disagree   *Strongly Agree*

- When I am calm, I believe I have the intelligence to understand and look for solutions.

1	2	3	4	5

Strongly disagree   *Strongly Agree*

- Unpleasant experiences are inevitable, but one does not need to fear them if Allah is with us.

1	2	3	4	5

Strongly disagree   *Strongly Agree*

Score 16 or higher- you're doing OK. Lower than 16, means you are struggling with self belief. Never fear, just keep working on the program and asking Allah for self belief. It will return, inshallah.

Exercise: Reassurance in Panic

Say Bismillah. Then say

'Remove the difficulty O Lord of mankind, and heal me. You are the Healer, no healing avails but Yours, a healing that leaves behind no ailment.'

Now read these facts- called affirmations- and appreciate their truth.

- No true panic ever killed anyone. All we ever have to do is just exist through it. And it will then just go when it is done.

- No embarrassment has any meaning in life. The only one who matters is Allah.

- We will try to learn skills to calm ourselves. They will work, given time. And if they don't so be it. We will keep trying, and maybe we will try something else. Allah knows what to do with us to guide us.'

- Panic is unpleasant. So we expect it to be unpleasant. That is all that panic ever is. It cannot hurt us any more than being unpleasant. Let it come. It cannot harm us beyond making me feel upset for a few minutes.

Write your own reassurances here if you like:

Reassurance for Social Anxiety

Say Bismillah. Then say

Remove the difficulty O Lord of mankind, and heal. You are the Healer, no healing avails but Yours, a healing that leaves behind no ailment.

Now read these out loud, and truly appreciate their truth. Take your time, reflect on them, repeat them. They will start to hit home.

- I fully expect to feel anxious. Feelings are feelings, and I can tolerate unpleasant feelings. They might be unpleasant, but they all pass.

- Nobody can ever control what other people think of them. Prophets and other great and pious people have suffered shame and embarrassment with gladness for the sake of Allah. If they can, then I can too, if that is what Allah has ordained for me for now.'

- Looking nervous is fine. Acting nervous is fine. I can tolerate those things. I can take a perspective on myself: I am one person, faulty and sinful, but my intentions are good. There is blessing in suffering if one has good intentions

Write your own reassurances here if you like:

Kitaabat-ul-Nafs: Giving voice to the Emotions

Your mind is part of you, designed to help you. However, sometimes you need to listen to it just like a doctor listens to your heartbeat. Does the pattern sound fine or does it sound troubled? Because worries are the main feature of anxiety, it's important to understand the pattern of what your Nafs is saying.

The Nafs prefers to use emotions, and these are not easily transformed into words. To understand yourself better, you need to help capture some emotions down on paper.

What sorts of things does your brain find itself worrying about?? Do certain worries come up more than others? What typically triggers your worries? How anxious do your worries make you?

In order to answer these questions, you need to get a good idea of what you worry about on a day-to-day basis. Kitaabat-ul-Nafs gives you a snapshot of your worries and you start to get to know that how your Nafs is so alarmed.

Exercise: Kitaabat-ul-Nafs: Making a note of worries.

AIM: To understand the nature of your worries

OUTCOME: Better understanding of how the worries happen.

TIME: 5 minutes a day, daily.

MATERIALS: A notebook, or diary, or your phone.

INSTRUCTIONS:

Track your worries several times a day for at least one week.

Not every worry, just three per day will do. The purpose is to get a snapshot of your worries. You can do this wherever you like- on your phone, in a basic diary. There are some blank forms after this example.

Sample Kitaabat-ul-Nafs

Date and time	Situation or trigger	Worry (what if?)	Anxiety (0 to 10)
Monday 7:30 a.m.	Planning a to-do list at breakfast	What if I don't get my work done today?	6
Monday 1.30 p.m.	Checking email messages: one from the boss.	What if it's bad news? I cant lose my job!	8
Monday 10 p.m.	Thinking about the driving test	What if I fail it? I will have wasted so much money learning	5

There are four columns in the form:

1. Date and time

2. Situation or trigger: What was going on when you started to worry.

3. The worry itself: Briefly describe the worry. Just write down your first few thoughts to provide a snapshot.

4. Anxiety (0 to 10): 0 means no anxiety. 5 is 'moderate' anxiety, and a rating of 10 means sheer overwhelming worry.

REMEMBER, FOR A GOOD KITAB AL-NAFS

Tip 1: KEEP IT SHORT. The Nafs drags you in with emotions, and you end up writing too much. Keep it short, just a few key words about the worry will do. People always write too much!

Tip 2: LISTEN TO YOUR BODY It's difficult to catch specific worries if you are worried all the time. One way is when you notice you get jittery, or feel butterflies in your stomach, or your breathing speeds up or you get sweaty. Ask yourself at that moment "What am I worrying about *right now*?"

Tip 3: DON'T HANG ABOUT: WRITE QUICKLY.

The Nafs doesn't think in words, so when you are emotional, you often forget what the emotion was about even a few minutes after it came and went. don't let it get away without grabbing what it says. Note the thought quickly! A voice note on your phone will be enough if you cant write immediately.

Kitaabat-ul-Nafs blank form

Date and time	Situation or trigger	Worry (what if?)	Anxiety (0 to 10)

Exercise: Recognizing Worry Types

Two types of worries can be described: current worries, and possible worries. The difference between the two is useful because the solutions are different. So try to see if you can tell which is which.

Activity: What type of worry is it?

1. *My mother is late coming home. What if she got hurt or attacked?*

   Tick which you think it is.

   Current worry

   Possible worry

2. *People are coming to eat but I haven't got enough food. If I go to the shop I might not have enough time to cook.*

   Current worry

   Possible worry

3. *I am quite overweight now. I really should try to get fit. But what if I can't find the time to exercise?*

   Current worry

   Possible worry

Not so easy sometimes, is it? To help decide, try asking if the problem a) has already taken place, and if b) you have any realistic control over it.

Using this logic, the worries above are thus:

1. *Possible worry. Your mother's accident is not confirmed and you have no control over such an event anyway.*

2. *Current worry. The issue is confirmed and you do have some control over the possible solutions. How you can get/ make extra food in time for your guests.*

3. *The trickiest one. Could be either, but we'll go for current problem. You have confirmed the weight issue and you are struggling to find the time to exercise. This solution is possibly within your control.*

After you've filled out your Kitaabat-ul-Nafs for one week, look over the worries and see if you can name each of the worries as current or possible.

Current worries need a system of finding solutions, and possible worries are addressed by a process of reality testing and rational exposure. More on this as we continue the program.

Thoughts, emotions and actions.

We attach meanings – attitudes - to our thoughts. When we do this, we give them some kind of emotional tint. The same thought can trigger very different emotions depending on the meanings we attach to it.

For example you see that your friend is ringing you. If you had an argument with the friend, you might believe that they are ringing to continue the argument and this makes you anxious. As a result you ignore the phone and avoid them. If you believe the friend was ringing to apologise and the call was going to be a good one, you would react completely differently. So the belief or meaning of a thought is what triggers emotion, and emotion then triggers a behaviour.

Why would we bother separating out meanings and interpretations of events? Because if we interpret something in a helpful way, it leads to more positive actions and outcomes. It is true that people who think in a more balanced way have happier lives, and this is one of the reasons. Allah makes it easy for us if we choose to see things in the way He wishes: balancing the negatives out with plenty of positives.

You need to consider that the Nafs is a powerful force, and depending on how we choose to guide it, it can actually work in our favour. We do this by using the Intellect. The intellect can introduce positive possibilities into a problem and once this happens, your brain cannot help but start thinking about them.

In life, what happens to us is often the result of our attitude to a situation. There are rich men who would talk to you as if they were poor, and there are poor men who talk as if they are wealthy in all the things they need. Neither of them is insane. They have the same brain functions as anyone else. The poorer man has learned to guide his mind to a more peaceful way of being, and in so doing, he actually does have a more pleasant life! Subhanallah.

If you want to learn about situations and stories like this, try my book 'Voyage of the Humble Soul. It is a short and poetic story about a young man who goes on Hajj, encountering many different types of people in a dream-like state of discovery.

Look at the next examples. Think them through in terms of thought>> emotion>>behaviour. The first one is completed for you. Positive reactions, and then negative reactions, are explored.

Situation 1: Habeeb, an old friend, invites you to come to their house. They want you to meet some of their new their friends. You don't know any of those folk yet.

Helpful thought: *Sounds good, alhamdulillah. I'll meet some new people and maybe make some new friends inshallah.*

Emotion: *Happy and excited*

Action: *I go to the house,, introduce myself to new people, and get to know them*

Unhelpful thought: Yikes*! No, I don't know anyone. It will be very awkward.*

Emotion: *Nervous and anxious*
Action: *I call Habeeb, make an excuse, and don't go. Or I do go, but I leave early.*

Exercise: Naming thoughts, emotions and actions

Situation 1: Your father is ill and he has asked you to run the family business for a while. You have to lead the employees and make decisions affecting them.

Positive thought: _____

Emotions: _____

Actions: _____

Negative thought: _____

Emotions: _____

Actions: _____

Situation 2: You rang an old friend to see how they were. They haven't rung back for several days.

Positive thought: _____

Emotions: _____

Actions: _____

Negative thought: _____

Emotions: _____

Actions: _____

Situation 3: You made plans with friends to go for food to a favourite place. You find out that they messed up your reservation so you have to find a new place. You do find one but none of you has eaten there before.

Positive thought: _____

Emotions: _____

Actions: _____

Negative thought: _____

Emotions: _____

Actions: _____

How to form the habit? REPETITION

Next time you face a dilemma of uncertainties, why not take the time to write down the positive and the negative thought options? This is just like getting into the workings of your brain, under the bonnet, and changing processes which have until now been rather gloomy, to brighter and more energetic ways of being.

It might look a little simple but it really does make so much sense when you write. You put feelings into words, and when you look back at your thoughts and feelings you can often be very surprised at how pessimistic you can become if you don't keep an eye on it. Writing gives you proof of what you were like.

You always have had the ability to think in a balanced way. All this exercise is doing is reminding you to reclaim helpful ways of seeing the world. Allah's grace and favours come in the form of dilemmas and opportunities sometimes: if we are determined to think about our options in a balanced way, we are more likely to spot His favours when they arrive. Set a time and date in your calendar to repeat this exercise if you like:

Recommendation: weekly.

Which day of the week? _____

What time? _____

Setting Goals for mastering anxiety

The worrying in your brain gets in the way of your life. It would be useful to know what you would like to get done in your life anyway, with or without your worrying. Inshallah your worries will reduce, but even if this is not in your destiny, you sometimes have to carry on. Nobody got too far waiting around for success to turn up!

Goals need to be concrete and clear, so that you know when you have achieved them. 'I want to be happy' is clear but not concrete. 'I would like to not feel so tired every morning' is better.

Don't worry about getting your goals perfect: they will probably change over time anyway. Just have a go at it. This whole process is about having a reasonable go. OK?

Exercise: Capturing some goals for mastering anxiety

There are different areas in life. Note down some goals if they apply to you.

Deen and spiritual life (e.g. being more on time with salah, being able to concentrate through salah better, reading a book on Hadith or Islamic History).

_____

_____

_____

Work and school (Getting a promotion, keeping your job in a crisis, succeeding in your exams)

_____

_____

Family and home life (spending more time with your siblings or kids, going out for a meal once a month, visiting a sick relative more often).

_____

_____

Individual learning and leisure (travelling to an interesting part of the country, or learning a new language.)

_____

_____

Your persona (Being more assertive, communicating more effectively, being more confident)

_____

_____

Other goals

Quite hard isn't it? Lots in one area, nothing in the other, unwieldy ideas, many competing priorities and desires. Now take a step back and be thankful that you made the effort, and also realise that you have been spelling out the multiple capabilities and gifts of freedom that Allah has given you. So many different things to try: it can be equally exhilarating or intimidating. With Allah in your heart, you can only do one thing: Get on, and try your best. You will win some, and lose others. This is a fact. Say bismillah and let's carry on.

Revising and revisiting your goals.

Recommendation: Every month.

Next date?   ------------

What time?   ------------

The Worry Testing Kit

Is it true that worries can be helpful? Yes it is true, potentially. Allah has told us that most things come with a positive and a negative, and worries are definitely part of this. We've seen how worries are really at root some kind of attempt at being alert to a situation, and a kind of blunt 'preparation' for challenge. This could help us get through a threat more easily, but it gets out of hand.

<u>'How helpful is this particular worry, and what does it say about me?'</u>

 With any worry we have, we can ask ourselves these questions:

a) What does the worry say about my basic values and morality or quality as a decent Muslim?

b) If I didn't worry about it, what would that say about my morality or qualities as a decent Muslim?

c) Could there be any benefit at all in having this worry, even to a small extent?

d) Does this worry lead me to take different actions than if I didn't have the worry? Are those actions helpful?

e) If I didn't worry about it, would something bad happen?

<u>Example:</u>

Suppose your worry was '*I worry that my children won't be hurt playing in the field*.....

Going through the worry testing kit (a) to (e)

a) That I love and care for my children.

b) I explore the possibilities of how they might be hurt and I make sure as much as possible that they are kept safe.

c) I am more alert to threats and can therefore spot them more easily.

d) I take time to alert my children to dangers themselves and to be safe and look out for each other.

e) I would neglect my children's safety and fail to teach them the value of caution and vigilance.

Exercise: The Worry Testing Kit

Go back to the worries you listed in your Kitaabat-ul-Nafs exercise. Note down two of your current worries here. Alternately list some different worries- up to you, no problem.

Worry 1

_____

Worry 2

_____

Now let's take a look at each one in turn. Can we find out if it comes from a good place?

So.... Go back to your two worries and answer the questions a to e in turn.

Worry 1: _____

a) What does the worry say about my basic values and morality or quality as a decent Muslim?

_____

_____

b) If I didn't worry about it, what would that say about my morality or qualities as a decent Muslim?

_____

_____

c) Could there be any benefit at all in having this worry, even to a small extent?

_____

_____

d) Does this worry lead me to take different actions than if I didn't have the worry? Are those actions helpful?

111

_____

----

e) If I didn't worry about it, would something bad happen?

_____

You might want to repeat this approach to remind yourself of the need to balance out your thinking from time to time.

Recommendation: weekly.

Which day of the week?   _____

What time?   _____

The wisdom of balanced thinking.

Notice we have always talked about balancing helpful and unhelpful interpretations and meanings, about pluses as well and minuses. Ignore the meaningless drivel about just seeing the positive side of things: this creates an artificial either/or situation.

Now then. It looks like we've cooked up a little problem for ourselves. In our effort to try to reduce worries, we have somehow ended up showing that the worries might actually be of benefit to us. Surely that can't be helpful?

Well, if there was a benefit to doing this exercise, what was it?

Have a think about the question, finding your answers, before reading these answers below. Done? Ok, read on.

a) Most worries come from a decent place. They are part of normal thought but they get out of hand. Worries are like water, or like fire, just like the Nafs. These are forces which can be useful in small amounts but harmful if they get out of hand.

b) It should emphasise to you that we are not interested in eliminating worries. We are interested in having the thoughts but at a reduced volume, and reduced frequency, so that we can actually get on with out lives. An anxiety state is when our processes to solve an issue have themselves become the problem that stops us from dealing with the problem effectively.

It's like a car which hasn't got any coolant or oil in it, so the engine is stuck: it can't get to the destination. There's nothing wrong with the destination, or the reason for going there. The problem is within car's attempt to move: its' own engine has got in the way. It needs to cool off, then it would get to where it needs to go more easily. In a way,, most anxiety is dealt with by this 'cooling off' process, and this workbook is all about exploring how to get that done as we go along.

In reality, you can have an engine and get to your destination without having to overheat every time. You don't need to associate your worries with your personality or values at all. You can still be a good person and solve problems without getting into an overheated state, alhamdulillah. Your mission is to detach yourself from the belief that problems can only be solved by worrying. In fact, they generally get made worse because the brain starts tripping over itself instead of dealing with the issue at hand.

Your True Self: Heart

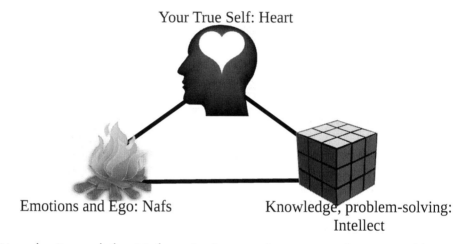

Emotions and Ego: Nafs   Knowledge, problem-solving:
                                          Intellect

You don't need the Nafs to ignite you into an anxiety state. You have the problem solving ability in your intellect, and the wisdom and Deen in your Heart, to solve any problems. The Nafs is only really there as an early signal; we are learning to deal with it and reassure it that the Intellect and Heart can take over solving the problem. We thank Allah for the Nafs' warning and we thank Allah for giving us different 'departments' in the brain which them specialise in moving us ahead with the solution. It would make little sense to leave the Nafs with the issue when we have such wonderful abilities in the Intellect and Heart. So let's make it a priority to stop, listen and hear what they have to say about an issue more in future.

Exercise: How would worrying less benefit me?

Let's spell out the benefits of being more in the coolness and wisdom of the Heart and Intellect more. Spell out how your life would improve. You might put the same answer down across several categories, and that's fine. If it is relevant, it is relevant. No need to write a novel. These are just rough ordinary notes.

How life would be better if I was less anxious:

My relationship with Allah and my practice of Deen would be improved in these ways:

_____

- -

My job or school life would be improved in these ways:

_____

- -

My character or personality would be improved in these ways:

_____

- -

Getting daily jobs and chores done would be improved in these ways:

_____

- -

My leisure and zest for life would be improved in these ways:

_____

- -

My ability to handle stress would be improved in these ways:

_____

My general wellbeing or happiness would be improved in these ways:

_____

Other areas of life would be improved in these ways:

_____

That was sort of fun wasn't it? Doesn't matter if it was hard: nothing amazing is achieved without a bit of struggle.

The Garden of Peace: RIADH

Understanding how to manage and take care of your Nafs- your emotional, primal side- is key in this section, which is a very different section to others.

The Nafs is non-verbal (doesn't tend to use words), instead relying on feelings, senses and instincts. It is also very closely connected to your physical body. So, to calm it, it is possible not to use words but to use the body.

The methods include both short term and long term strategies. All are concerned with connecting to your physical or spiritual self, taking you away from the volume of thoughts and voices in your head, to a place of calm.

Mankind cannot bear too much thinking. Alhamdulillah, Allah has considered this and given us numerous methods to bring a curtain of soft peace to our minds if wee pay attention to our physical body in certain ways such as nutrition, breathing and exercise, and in spiritual ways such as Salah, Ruqya and seeking Refuge in His cloak.

Exercise: Finding RIADH, The garden of peace (RIADH).

This is a deep breathing and visualisation technique which I have borrowed from Instant Actions. A similar approach can also be found on my YT channel, called 'How to be a Mindful Geyser'.

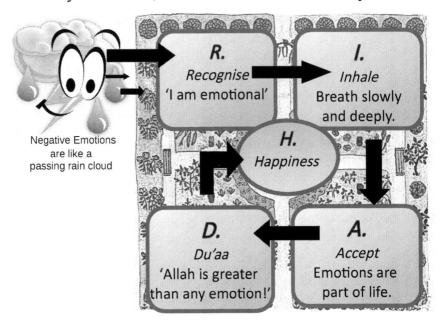

Recognise
Recognise that you are being visited by emotion. Give it some respect. Name it! Say 'I am angry', 'I am anxious' or whatever it is. Greet the guest with a name. It immediately starts to settle.

Inhale
In the second garden, you inhale, slowly and deeply. Taking slow breaths, using all your chest and belly, directly feeds back soothing signals to your Nafs. It is astonishing how much slow breathing can actually calm the mind. Just concentrate on the breathing, for a couple of minutes. Everything else can wait.

Accept

Even unpleasant emotions must be accepted. You don't need to know why the emotion is there. You must simply just accept it. It is in your garden, and it is part of you. Do the cloud a great favour: don't fight it off. It is simply bringing rain. You are trying to be a peaceful and reasonable person, but to do so means you accept the parts of you that are unreasonable. This way, they don't have a hold of you. Every garden needs rain: sometimes rain comes in a storm. Just hold fast and it passes.

Du'aa- Say Alhamdulillah!

Thank Allah for your emotions, use them if they are useful, but just let them pass if they are not. Storm-clouds can have good or bad effects, just like your Nafs: it depends how you are prepared to accept them. The more you welcome it, the better you will get at dealing with it. Be patient and kind with yourself. You are designed in a way that is perfect in the way Allah intended.

Happiness

At the centre of the garden is a pool: this is where the rain can fall and drain away. Happiness is now restored. You can now move on; the waters are calm. Get on with what you were doing before the emotion came to disturb you.

If you have practised this method, then you will probably be feeling a lot more settled by now. If not, then it doesn't matter. Emotions are only emotions. Take it easy; practise the technique again at some point. No need to lambast yourself for not getting it perfect. These things take time. The brain is a very plastic entity, meaning it changes slowly, over weeks and months, when you practice something, becoming steadily better the more you do it.

A tip: Try forcing a smile and imagine a happy time. Evidence suggests that when people imagine being happy, and when they force an artificial smile, this has been shown to recreate the emotion in a genuine sense.

119

Remembering a better future

What a strange title. How can anyone remember a time in the future? Well, let me explain.

For those of us who have been lost in worry for a long time, we could say that we have transported ourselves away from the present time. We imagine both the past and the future. Both of these things are 'visualised' in the memory. Memory is reinforced by repetition, and sooner or later, these visions become the only ones we have. In effect, we have forgotten what it was like to imagine better times, future or past.

So this exercise is about balancing your memory by bringing those visions back. When we are in 'a good place' mentally, *sucoon* (an Arabic/ middle eastern word for a sort of sweet peacefulness, almost a child-like state) is found. When this happens, we can think in more settled ways. The Nafs is becalmed. These things thrive when you are in a state of play: dealing with challenges as if they are part of a positive game rather than a burdensome threat.

A worry free life. What would I do with it?

Let your mind feel light; dare yourself to have happy playful thoughts. Allah is happy when his creatures are happy, and He gave us the ability to have dreams and hopes for very good reason, yet we as adults don't use this ability because we confuse being serious with being solemn.

What a shame. It makes no sense to not use a good, wholesome ability that Allah has given you, which was evident when when you were a baby. It doesn't disappear; you just forget it. It doesn't matter if your ideas are fanciful or even a little bit ridiculous. It matters just that you believe that happiness starts in the mind.

Exercise: Remembering a better future.

How would mastery over worry improve your life?

I have listed categories here, and in brackets, I have listed some ideas. Try to make your own, or bother some of the examples given. Either way, make a note of what you think.

Deen and Spirituality (I would feel totally loved and welcomed by Allah, as if all my decisions were 100% supported and endorsed by the Almighty, always under his protection, etc)

_____

_____

At my job or school life (e.g. I would be promoted to boss or prefect because of my apparent composure and wisdom,)

_____

_____

My character or personality: (I would be closer to my Rules of Conduct- see Instant Insights or Youtube for this. More honourable, better reputation with others.)

_____

_____

Daily jobs and chores: (My chores are a, b and c. I would get them done with much less effort/ better timing/ take on more etc)

_____

_____

Leisure and zest for life (I would take up studying something, learn about the Prophet, build that little house on some land, travel the world with a quest to learn about Islam in different places, etc)

_____

121

My ability to handle stress:

_____

My general wellbeing or happiness: (My sense of freedom, my confidence, my connection to others, my sense of purpose and goals).

_____

Other areas of life:

_____

Repetition: To re-read these notes. When you are mid-way through any program, or when you feel you are worn down from all the effort you are making to master anxiety. Replenish your goals, imagine your future more boldly: it energises and reassures the Nafs that the changes you are making are worth it.

Recommendation: Weekly, after Esha on a given night.

Which day of the week?   _____

What time?   _____

Using the Mind's Court of judgment

Aims:
-To understand in detail, the way the Intellect and Heart can examine a worry rationally and wisely.
- To use 'reasonable arguments' to take a worry apart.

Your Deen, your true character: Heart

Emotions and Ego: Nafs

Knowledge, problem-solving: Intellect

The Intellect is a great stickler for accuracy and truth. It is interested in facts, logic, and getting to the truth in a calm and step by step way. This is useful when it comes to calming the Nafs down and making our thoughts more reasonable, but the Intellect is slower and more demanding of our mental energy, so we have to give it time and space to think.

One way the Intellect can come in handy is as a little 'court' where the **facts for and against** are put forward, so a final judgement can be made.

'Fahas-ul-Nafs': Examination of the Nafs, for and against.

This exercise has 2 steps:

A. You look for FACTS and EVIDENCE that are in favour of, and against, a worry. We ask questions which test our assumptions.

B. Then this collection of facts and evidence is passed to your Heart, your Highest self, to form an overall summary and judgment.

Let's look at step A.

1. The case against worry has these reasonable arguments:

- **Worrying does not make me automatically a moral person**

- **Worry doesn't really help with problem solving**

- **Worry doesn't help with motivation**

Looking at these testing assumptions with some examples:

Example: *I worry for my children's safety because I am a moral, conscientious person.*

- **Worrying does not make me automatically a moral person**

Let's look for FACTS and EVIDENCE.

Question: Does worrying about my children's safety really show that I'm a good parent?

Answer: No. I often do things to protect my children's safety without worry, like I hold their hands when we cross the street.

Question: Do I know someone with this positive trait who doesn't worry? If so, how does that person show this trait? They show they care just by being positive and loving.

Answer: Sabiha is a great parent. Yet she doesn't seem to worry as much as me, if at all. She makes it look effortless somehow. She's just very loving.

Question: Have I ever seen my worry as a negative personality trait?

Answer: Sometimes I am so worried that I don't enjoy my time with my children.because I'm preoccupied with worries. I get irritable or impatient.

Question: Have others ever told me that my worry is a negative personality trait?

Answer: My children have told me that I often seem preoccupied or distracted. They sometimes get upset, as do I, when I have snapped at them verbally.

- **Worry doesn't really help with problem solving**

125

Example: *Worrying about work allows me to predict problems and solve them quickly.*

Question: Do I actually solve my problems or am I just dwelling on them?

Answer: Most of my worries about problems at work aren't about real problems. They aren't yet real and mostly don't happen. And even if they were real, I dwell on problems, not solutions.

Question: Has worrying about my problems ever interfered with my ability to solve them? Have I ever procrastinated or avoided dealing with problems because of worry?

Answer: Often I've gotten so worried and anxious about problems at work that I actually avoided dealing with the situation, or ask someone else to deal with it.

I have got so worried before that it actually led to my slowing down and getting less done.

- **Worry Doesn't help with Motivation**

Example: *Worrying about my salah motivates me to pray it on time and not miss it.*

Question: Do I know people who pray salah on time without worrying?

Answer: Rashid just seems to go to and from the masjid in a totally relaxed way. If he misses salah, he just catches up, no fuss.

Question: Has this worry ever interfered with my ability to accomplish things?

Answer: I get so worried in salah that I get distracted and can't remember which rakat I am in. I lose my place.

Question: Do I ever avoid or put off doing things I'm worried about, rather than becoming motivated to do them?

2025 DR TK HARRIS

Answer: I procrastinate with chores and bills because I get stressed about getting them done properly or not being able to afford the bills. This just makes the whole thing worse, I know, but it still happens. It's irrational!

2. The case in support of the worry has these reasonable arguments:

- **Worry Provides Protection from Negative Emotions**

- **Worry Can Prevent Negative Outcomes**

So let's take each point in turn again:

- **Worry Provides Protection from Negative Emotions**

Example: *Worrying about the health of my parents prepares me for the sadness if they do pass away.*

Let's look for FACTS and EVIDENCE.

Question: Has this strategy actually worked out well in the past?

Answer: I used to worry about my toys breaking when I was a kid. So I never played with them too much. Then when I got older I actually regretted that. I should have played more carefree.

Question: When you had an unexpected bad thing that you didn't worry about before, did you cope with it OK?

Answer: When my bike wheel broke on the way home once, I dealt with the issue OK. Asked one of the people in a nearby house if he could lend me a spanner, and he helped me out.

In my daily life, how do I feel emotionally when I worry about bad things that could happen?

Answer: I actually feel quite miserable when I worry.

- **Worry Can Prevent Negative Outcomes**

Question: Are there times when worrying actually made things

127

worse?

Answer: I was so worried about not doing well in my da'wah class that I ended up leaving the course.

Question: Do I have examples of times when good things happened even though you didn't worry?

Answer: On several occasions people turn up at the house unannounced. Because there is no warning I actually am more relaxed and don't fret about what to do for them so much. I have a more pleasant time.

Step B: Finding a way forward by presenting the evidence as a whole to the Heart.

Looking back at the answers, it seems as if you have got a neat collection of really helpful facts and evidence, which we arrived at quite calmly and reasonably, when we looked for them. Sometimes the way forward becomes clear while we are answering: we discover something helpful and suddenly the sense of worry just 'drops' away. This is a breakthrough moment, when the emotions have been schooled into calm.

Sometimes this doesn't happen, but we can still look at how far we have got with gratitude, and then mull over the facts and evidence calmly in salah, making du'aa and telling Allah about it, and sleeping on it. It is this process of making a calm and steady effort that brings us victory over worry.

Exercise: Fahas-ul-Nafs. Examination of a worry

Write down a worry:

_____

_____

Now answer the following.

1. *The case against the worry*

Can someone still be a decent and good Muslim and deal with this worry without it taking over their life? Yes or No.

_____

_____

So can you think of other people who have conquered a similar problem without worrying so much, while still being good people morally?

_____

_____

Could this worry actually be a destructive or harmful thing to me?

_____

_____

Does the worry actually solve the problem? Yes or No.

_____

_____

Do I end up dwelling on the problems rather than the solutions?

Does the worry drain my motivation and energy? Yes or No

So is it possible that I am too motivated, therefore always worried? If I were a bit more relaxed could I actually get on with action?

Does worry actually help me get things done or does it make me procrastinate?

Does worry protect me from feeling low?

Yes/ No/ Don't Know

If a bad thing happened that was unexpected, could I deal with it effectively, proving that I didn't need to worry about it beforehand as such?

Yes/ No/ Don't Know.

Overall, what is the emotional consequence of worry on my enjoyment and effectiveness in life?

Does worrying actually guarantee to prevent bad things happening?

Yes/ No/ Don't know

Is it possible that I could succeed at something without having worried about it as such?

Is the worry having an overall positive or negative effect on my relationships with family and friends?

Yes/ No/ Don't know

Is the worry having an overall negative effect on my self esteem?

Yes/ No/ Don't know

Is the worry having an overall negative effect on the quality of my other tasks and activities of life?

Yes/ No/ Don't know

Is there a physical effect on me through worrying? Palpitations, sweatiness, poor sleep, appetite problems, upset stomach, that sort of thing?

Yes/ No/ Don't know

Is the worry having an overall negative effect on my energy levels?

Yes/ No/ Don't know

b. The case in support of the worry

Can I recall times when this worry led me to act in a positive way?

Can I think of other people who thanked me for worrying about this issue?

Could this worry actually be a positive personality trait for me to have?

Has worry actually solved problems for me in the past?

What times were there when worrying about this issue helped me to solve it better?

Has worrying ever given me a boost of energy and motivation to solve this issue?

Was I too relaxed before? Has worrying prompted me to act?

Are there times when worrying about a similar issue made me more prepared for it when things did turn out bad in the end?

Does worry protect me from feeling low?

Yes/ No/ Don't know

Does worrying actually guarantee to prevent bad things happening?

Yes/ No/ Don't know

Can I remember things that I have failed at because I didn't worry about them enough?

Is the worry having an overall positive effect on my relationships with family and friends?

Yes/ No/ Don't Know

Is the worry having an overall positive effect on my self esteem?

Yes/ No/ Don't Know

Is the worry having an overall positive effect on the quality or completion of my other tasks and activities of life?

Yes/ No/ Don't Know

Is there a beneficial physical effect on me through worrying? Am I eating more healthily, sleeping better, in generally better shape?

Yes/ No/ Don't Know

Is the worry having an overall positive effect on my energy levels?

Yes/ No/ Don't Know

Come back to do Fahas-al-Nafs again and again. Practice, redo, re-examine. Just like nobody ever just reads Quran the once and them moves on, you need to nurture the wisdom you have learned by repeating it, especially in times of crisis. The brain, especially the Intellect, gets better with practice, increasing its speed and wisdom the more you walk it along the same good path.

The Heart: Keeper of Truths and Wisdom.

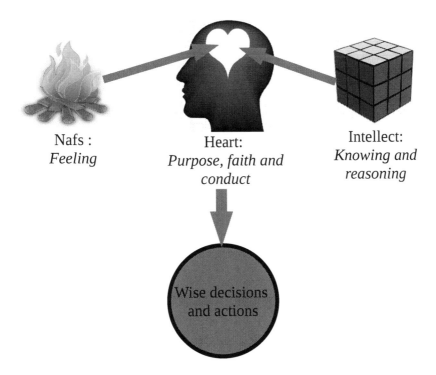

Nafs :
Feeling

Heart:
Purpose, faith and conduct

Intellect:
Knowing and reasoning

Wise decisions and actions

Your Highest True self is your Heart. This is the conscious version of you, who has to take a judgment going forward.

Look at the previous exercise. Reflect on the positives and negatives of each point in turn. When you are done, come back here and read the next paragraphs.

If you reach a point where you have positives and negatives for each, you have reached an integrated, wiser truth: that everything in life has positives and negatives. That there are plusses and minuses. Sometimes the positives outweigh the negatives, sometimes the other way, sometimes it isn't clear.

The wiser truth above all this are thus:

- A little bit of worry is useful.

- In anxious people the amount of worry gets out of hand.

- Questioning it for the evidence gives you a sense of balance.

- You can move forward knowing that you have not abandoned the worry but that you have got closer to a truth

- Most of life is unknowable. We simply do our best about a situation, and worrying may or may not help, but it will wear us down if we do it too much.

- Better to aim for less worry, not being free from it altogether.

- More often, worried people believe their worries help them when in fact they can be helping or hindering.

- It feels more realistic and less pressured, to aim to worry less than to be totally free from it.

- Again, the Nafs is like fire or water. It is better to have fire or water and know how to deal with them, rather than let them control or harm us. We would also suffer if we didn't have them at all.

Complex issues sometimes benefit from quiet contemplation, discussion with a friend or loved one, or talking to Allah about. Sleeping on an issue over a few days also helps the mind to come to an answer that isn't immediately obvious. Trust yourself to find a judgment. This takes practice if you are a professional worrier, but it does chip away at your old habits over time. Keep faith in yourself, as much as Allah has faith in you.

Different Reactions to anxiety

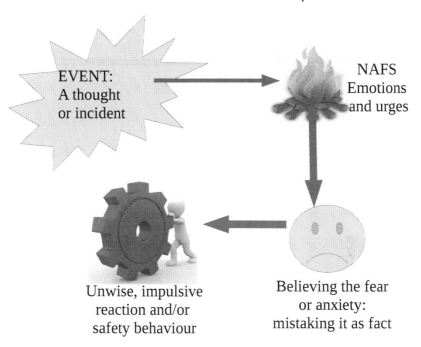

EVENT:
A thought
or incident

NAFS
Emotions
and urges

Unwise, impulsive
reaction and/or
safety behaviour

Believing the fear
or anxiety:
mistaking it as fact

If the Heart or Intellect are not involved, or not strong enough, we react to events (thoughts or incidents in life) through the Nafs. The result is an almost instinctive, reactive course of action. This is intended to keep us safe but can end up being a very troublesome habit. Let's list them here.

Reassurance seeking
It might feel embarrassing but we keep asking someone else to make sure that something is OK. Like we don't trust our own judgment.

Multiple checking
Making sure the doors are locked, that the car is always totally full of fuel, or supervising a colleague to make sure they don't forget something (micro-managing them).

137

Over-informing
Not moving forward with a decision, but instead just trying to research all the options to the point where even the smallest things seem to have relevance. To other people it seems we are confusing and overwhelming ourselves with information that is not really material to the decision.

Avoiding
Simply not participating. Cancelling an event which might cause anxiety. Not mixing with new people, or avoiding people whom you might upset or feel harshly judged by. Ducking out of commitments.

Procrastination
It's a powerful illusion where we decide to put something off. We convince ourselves that we will do it later. That 'later' never comes, or we leave things til too late, and do a bad job, thus making us worry even more in future.

Weak involvement
We commit partially to something, for example a walking trip with friends, giving ourselves the option to step out. The problem is we never get properly involved and end up feeling like a passenger in the event, or other people find us difficult to enthuse.

Impulsive actions
Leaving things to a roll of the emotional dice. We mistake this for 'gut feeling' and intuition, but gut feeling only works once we have true experience of life and we can truly see everything involved. Otherwise it's nothing more than a baseless whisper which leads us away from the truth.

Are you really in control of your actions?

When we do things with the Nafs in charge, we are acting out of emotion rather than true judgment. It could be said that we are not representing ourselves properly. We haven't calmly applied our logic, Deen or wisdom to the issue. As such, we fall into a behaviour which may take hold as a senseless or silly a habit but we find that we can't break free from it: after all, if we live life just to satisfy emotions, we are only using one third of the true Muslim mind.

These habits or actions, if they become recognisable patterns, are sometimes called *safety behaviours*.

All such habits bring some kind of small, immediate reward or relief. Reactions coming only from the Nafs are an attempt to deal with a worrisome emotion or thought. They seem to solve the emotional burden for a short while, which is why they become a habit. But they maintain the cycle of worry overall. This is because they prevent you from really being involved in your life, from taking decisive action which is informed by your Intellect or your Heart. You have not let the actual facts, or your true character, shine through because the Nafs has hijacked you and convinced you to move too quickly.

Identifying this kind of thing is exactly what you do to get control of the situation. Remember, the Nafs is not your enemy but it can lead you to do things that bring you harm if you don't respond to it in a more systematic way, examining it more calmly with your Intellect and your Heart before coming to a decision.

139

Exercise: Identifying our own reactions to anxiety

Look at this table as an example

Situation	Worry (what if?)	Reaction
Starting a new class	What if it's no good? What if I can't understand it?	**Avoiding the class**
Abdul texted; said we should meet up to talk.	What if he's going to say something bad? What if I've upset him?	I mulled over all the things he said and re-read all our texts. **(Multiple checking).**
I need to buy a new computer	What if it's not the right one? What if it turns out to be a waste of money?	Spending weeks researching the specs of all possible computers, and becoming bogged down **(Over-informing).**

Now do this for yourself. Look over the list in the previous chapter to see if you are using any of the types listed.

Situation	Worry (what if?)	Reaction

Becoming wise about worries
(Tajriba-tul-Hikmah)

The Nafs works by using *approximations, impressions, and exaggerations.* We react by imagining scenarios which are therefore worse than reality.

So, we need to develop some ways of reacting less extremely. In other words, we need to try out what kind of actions would actually serve us better in future. To do this, we take a worry or fear, and test it out to see if it is actually truthful. Possible outcomes are:

a) If the worry is true, that's fine: we then see what we do about that outcome. We see if we can react in a wise way when we face the situation. The chances are thing will turn out far less badly than our Nafs would have us believe.

b) If it is untrue, we have gained the truth about the worry and we can tell the Nafs to calm down and it will probably listen much better once we show it the facts. It may take time to settle down: one of the weird things about the Nafs is that you can still have the emotions about something even if that thing is no longer relevant. It's quick to get fired up, but often slow to let go.

At each stage of testing out the worry, you rate your emotions out of 10 each time, 10 being the most unpleasant.

Example
I worry that I will not be able to find all the things I need in the store when I go shopping, then I will panic in the store. I will be embarrassed and upset. 10/10 unpleasant.

Experiment:
I'll go shopping for five things and see if I can find them.

My worry predicts:
I wont find the items and I will panic; I'll be upset and disappointed.

When I actually did it successfully:
I found all five items. It was a little bit nerve racking, but I kept wandering around, stopped for a deep breath and prayed a few du'aa for Allah to help me stay calm, and it worked.
Anxiety 3/10 nice and low.

Coping: A bit of du'aa, and some deep breaths, and I was fine.

Outcome: I have faith in Allah but didn't think to actually just pray and ask him for help when panicking. Turns out he helped me out when I reached out!

When I actually failed:
I found three items, then prayed a few du'aa, took some breaths, but simply couldn't find the remaining two. I walked around getting more worried. I left the store. Nobody seemed to notice my panicking; it was all 'inside' I guess, and when I decided to leave, I immediately felt better. Anxiety 6/10 in the middle but not as bad as expected.

Coping:
I left the store. I've learned that even if I fail, nothing too terrible happens. Funny how my Nafs would have me believe otherwise. Shaytan really does play mischief in the mind doesn't he?

The key questions to ask in Tajriba-tul-Hikmah are therefore:
• *Did the situation lead to a negative outcome?*
Yes and no. One time I got what I wanted, and the other time I didn't.
• *If a negative outcome occurred, how bad was it?*
It actually wasn't that bad. I didn't really panic as such, I had the presence of mind to just leave.
• *If a negative outcome occurred, how did you cope?*
A little bit flustered, but I really did feel better when I stopped and asked for Allah's help. He always does what is best for me, so it was better for me to leave the store. I accept that as a Muslim with total satisfaction.

Everyone finds behavioural experiments difficult at first, but many people report that they quickly become rewarding, alhamdulillah. At the very least, you are able to step outside of yourself and deal with the problem a bit more like what it actually is: a health issue. It's an opportunity to learn and strengthen yourself. It is by no means a defect in your character.

<u>Design your own wisdom experiments</u>

Here's some examples of experiments that deal with underlying worries. See if you can imagine what worries the person had, that led them to try these experiments.
• Going to a new place to eat with new friends
• Buying a small ($20 worth) computer accessory after looking online for only one hour rather than a full day.
• Deciding what to wear without asking for reassurance from my sister.
• Calling a friend I have not spoken to in some years.
• Going to the grocery store to buy just three things, without a list
• Not checking my social media for one full hour.
• Sitting at my computer without looking at games/ recreation

These tests require a bit of thought and planning. Here's some tips:

1. Start small, unambitious, simple.

2. Make the goals as clear as you can.

3. Write down your plan somewhere.

4. Rate your anxiety out of ten.

5. See it as an experiment: failure is just a type of feedback; a sign to repeat the experiment at that level, not to go up a level yet.

6. Expect to feel anxious. That's the whole point; feeling anxiety but not reacting in the old negative way. Just staying the course, staying steady.

7. Move up a ladder of achievement. Place the highest achievement at the top (e.g. going to the store and buying 20 items without leaving or getting panicked) and then design some intermediate steps up towards that high point.

So the first step could be 'going to the store and just coming out again without buying anything at all'. Once you've succeeded in that, you take stock, make a note, and next time (perhaps the next day) you follow the next step: going to the store and buying two things, then leaving. And so on.

If you dont get past any given step, just wait til your next date and try it again. No need to overthink it: this whole process relies more on behaviour than internal reflection.

145

Exercise: Becoming wise about worries
Tajriba-tul-Hikmah

Time to do it on your own:
Name a worry:

_____

_____

How much worry does that cause you out of 10?

_____

What would be the ultimate successful experiment- the highest success of that worry. Something you can aspire to doing.

_____

_____

Now list four little experiments you can do to work up to that ultimate aim.

1._____

2._____

3._____

4._____

5.(Ultimate aim)_____

Repetition: Recommendation: variable frequency, but must be regular, Can be done every day or once a week, moving up one step at a time.

How often will you be doing these? Name a date, day or regular time slot to do them:

_____

Now look at the first of the experiments, and write down the expected anxiety level out of ten.

Tip: this score should be between 3 and 7: not too low, not too high, but bearable.

Date:

Aim: _____

Anticipated anxiety

_____

Successful or not?

_____

How did I cope? Did I discover something new, think on my feet, etc?

_____

Actual anxiety rating out of 10:

_____

Other comments or plans for the next experiment:

_____

For repetition, you could use a table like the one on the next page. Depending on the experiment, you could repeat it once a day, or once a week, whatever you find practical and keeps you at the 'bearable' level of anxiety, neither too relaxed nor too tense.

Experiment and date:	Predicted outcome	Actual outcome	How I coped	Anxiety rating
1.				
2.				
3.				
4.				
5. Ultimate aim				

Taking stock of progress

So we've come this far. Sunhanallah. Let me tell you this: you have already learned FAR more than most other people know about how the mind works. This will serve you very well inshallah. Over time, as you repeat it and let it sink in, this will show itself. Sometimes your new strength isn't apparent until you face a new situation or test. Then it becomes very pleasant to see how far you have come along.

Sit back and give thanks to Allah. We've identified certain issues which cause us worry, and worked out some of the patterns we fall into which seem to solve the emotional problem in the short term but actually make us more stressed in the long term.

Alhamdulillah, many people start to discover that their beliefs and worries are indeed exaggerated. The Nafs is cheeky and difficult to tame this is our lifelong test.

You pass, you fail, you win some, you lose some. Generally, when you pay attention to yourself and bring your Intellect and Heart into the equation, you are using the parts of the brain that have until now been quiet. You may not even have known that they are separate parts. In all cases, you head towards a better understanding of yourself and a discovery that negative experiences are just that: experiences. They need not dictate your life, and they are far less negative if you approach them with calmness and faith in Allah to help you out.

149

Exercise: Taking stock of our progress so far

So, let's take stock. Ask yourself the following questions to assist you in taking stock of your experiences:

• I've noticed positive changes in my life since I started learning about my mind, and doing these exercises.

1	2	3	4	5
Disagree totally			Agree totally	

• Situations that used to be scary are now more doable.

1	2	3	4	5
Disagree totally			Agree totally	

• I have more free time and or get things done more quickly

1	2	3	4	5
Disagree totally			Agree totally	

• I feel more confident in my ability to read and understand my emotions and navigate my way to calmer thinking and options for action.

1	2	3	4	5
Disagree totally			Agree totally	

• I worry less

1	2	3	4	5
Disagree totally			Agree totally	

Get Videos & Books, Raise Funds drtkharris.wordpress.com

• There have been improvements in my physical signs of anxiety arousal such as sleep, irritability, muscle tension, or feeling restless.

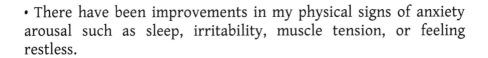

1	2	3	4	5
Disagree totally				Agree totally

• Others in my life notice a positive change in me.

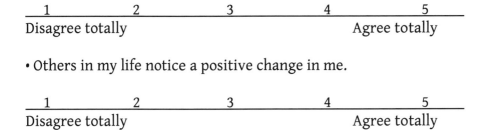

1	2	3	4	5
Disagree totally				Agree totally

The positive feelings arising from this are also wonderful: it's not all misery and gloom with the Nafs you know! When you achieve something, tha Nafs gives you a warm 'buzz' of happiness. It feels righteous pride. Your mind feels more integrated because you are using more of it! Facing uncertainty, as Allah has told us, has benefit to us all.

Repetition Recommendation: Check in with yourself about every 2 weeks when you are starting out, and every 6 weeks once you are getting more settled.

How often will you be doing these?

Date and time you can next check in:_____

Test occasion / date	1	2	3	4	5	6	7	8
Score								

Alhamdulillah: seeing the opportunity in crisis

'With carefulness you realise your opportunity'

-Arab proverb.

We are told for sure that problems have benefit in them for us. We are also told that we must use our minds and creativity, and our abilities and character, to try to solve problems and identify ways forward for ourselves. This is why we are also told to say Alhamdulillah when facing any problem, disastrous to minor: there is something in it waiting for us to learn, grow or solve.

It is true to say that those who view problems as opportunities tend to solve them more easily. This is because problem solving is affectively sensitive: influenced by your mood. The more you are positive, the more persistent you are and the more creative you can be. Think about babies and children: they only really learn by experimenting and playing with things, and yet, within a year, the average newborn has gone from basically bedridden to walking, talking a new language, and understanding the basics of human interactions!

We can learn therefore that the brain works better when we see problems as chances to fix something in a new or better way.

Threats and opportunities can be seen as two extremes on a single line. Problems are rarely 100 percent threatening, or 100 percent an opportunity.

We tend to see problems as somewhat threatening, which makes sense; problems are by definition something that needs to be sorted out. But there is gold to be found in this dirt.

Zed is worried because he had an argument with Khalid. He thinks Khalid might be angry with him even though some time has passed. Zed is scared to approach Khalid.

However, there are also opportunities here. For example, if Zed addressed the issues with Khalid their friendship could grow stronger. Zed could improve his communication skills and empathy. Neither of these opportunities makes the scariness disappear, but they give Zed a more balanced view of the situation. This gives him a greater nudge to get on and start to solve the issue.

Exercise: Finding the reasons to say Alhamdulillah.

Choose a problem that's particularly troublesome for you and write it down. You can pick one of the original ones you wrote down in your kitaabat-ul-Nafs, if you like. Or choose a different one.

----

1. Next, rate how negative the situation seems to you using a scale from 0 to 100 percent fear factor.

2. Say Alhamdulillah, and thank Allah for the problem. Know that there is opportunity within it. Think of any number of possible opportunities that this problem raises. Write them down. Relax: ideas will come if you invite them. One way is to pray a really peaceful, slow Nafl salah, and when in sujood, ask Allah to help you to come up with realistic opportunities that the situation might hold for you. After Salah, write the ideas down as they come. Don't worry, they will come, often sooner than you think. You have said alhamdulillah: this opens the floodgates to the wisdom that Allah has invested within you.

A tip: Write opportunities that make sense to you. If you are struggling, just imagine a really creative person or friend, or indeed, talk to such a person. Enter your question online: chances are someone else has encountered it and written about it too. Imagine you had a good friend in the same situation. How would you advise them? List every possible opportunity, even silly ones, to get the brain going.

3. Now you have some possible benefits. Re-rate how threatening the situation now seems to you, again from 0 to 100 percent.

The point is this: sometimes the opportunity makes the threat seem less scary, sometimes not. But in every single case, you have found an opportunity: you have brought some sense of balance.

Sample problem: *My mother has taken ill and I should go and see her. But that means I won't be able to attend to my business.*
Threat rating: *90 percent fear factor.*

Opportunities:
-*Maybe once I'm at my mum's I can ring around to see if someone can recommend a good worker to come and help me at the store.*
-*Maybe my cousin, who has lost his job, could help out?*
New threat rating: *50 percent fear.*

Now try some yourself
Problem 1:

_____

Fear factor (0 to 100%):

_____

Opportunities:

_____

New fear factor (0 to 100%):

_____

Problem 2:

_____

Fear factor (0 to 100%):

_____

Opportunities:

_____

New fear factor (0 to 100%):

_____

155

Solving real problems

Some of our anxieties are actual real concerns. They require actual solutions.

Your True Self: Heart

Emotions and Ego: Nafs   Knowledge, problem-solving:
                                              Intellect

Our Intellect appreciates that the problem is a real one that needs to be solved. Financial worries are typical of this. If I have no money and no obvious means of getting it, then my anxieties about my future grow larger and my Nafs can quickly dominate my mind because of the harmful consequences of being penniless. The Intellect struggles to make progress because the problem itself causes so much emotional upheaval in the Nafs, that ironically, some people find themselves unable to think in a calm manner.

The issue here is that we need to get on and think up solutions. It's hard to do that when the mind is stressed out, so it's no surprise that so many people can develop serious mental health issues when they have money worries. How can one approach the issue so that it doesn't seem so overwhelming?

One of the ways is to break the task down into smaller steps. To break the worry down into smaller, more manageable worries. Being jobless is a big deal, but there are so many steps to finding work. From getting up, to eating, to getting qualified, and so on. In turn, is it really a job that one wants, or is the problem about what the job provides- money?

It's a question of these steps:
1. Find the real issue behind the worry.
2. Define a goal which addresses that real issue.
3. Generate solutions, and pick the most reasonable sounding ones.
4. Prepare to shift and try new or other solutions rapidly.
5. If still no joy, then start back at the beginning and persist. Every time, say Alhamdulillah for the problem, then Bismillah as you set out.

1. Find the real issue behind the worry.

You might think your problem is that you don't have a job. The real issue is that you are running out of money. This is important to know, because money can be raised in multiple ways, not just by having a job. So immediately, your sense of panic begins to reduce because you have opened up the possible variety of solutions.

2. Define the goal which addresses the real issue.

S.M.A.R.T. defines a good goal: It is specific, measurable, achievable, realistic, and timely.

So the goal you have is how to raise money. To make it clearer, work out how much, and by when. In emergencies, the main aim is to get enough to pay off your main expenses for the next month or so. So you add up your expenses and arrive at a reasonable, minimum figure to get through the next month.

3. Generate solutions, and pick the most reasonable sounding ones.

So now you have to create solutions. There are many more ways of gaining money than just getting a job. Jobs provide steady money but thy are hardly the only way to raise emergency cash. Supposing your industry is in a slump due to COVID or something similar, so no jobs can be found. How do you raise money? Doing odd jobs in the neighbourhood. Selling off some unwanted things. Asking your parents or relatives for a short term advance. Now the ideas come forward.

When generating solutions, keep this in mind:
a) Write a whole lot of them down. Doesn't matter how ridiculous they sound. The point is to get that creative machine going.
b) Calm your Nafs directly. Make du'aa, slow yourself down by making calm, humble salah, find an inspirational speech online, read about other people who have struggled over hardship. The Hadith are a good start, but there are millions of other places to find examples. Reassure your Nafs that you have the guts to try something, and help the Nafs along by calming it. Try slow breathing (exercises later in this program, on my YT channel and other books). When you are less panicked, your Nafs releases your intellect to playing more creatively with solutions.

c) Prefer solutions that are clear steps, rather than vague ones. Meaning for example 'Take all old clothes out of the attic to see which ones can be sold online' rather than 'be more positive about selling stuff.'

d) Think about your core strengths as a person. What do you do naturally that other people find difficult? There is a clue as to your real value lies in the world of work and money. If you can attach your solutions to your natural strengths somehow, then you are much more likely to succeed. My book Instant Actions has a lot of detail about finding your strengths as a person.

Give yourself a time limit and a clear plan of specific steps to take. Questions, jobs, to-dos: write them down on a daily list. Check them off when done, and implement the solution (s) that you have chosen.

4. Prepare to shift and try new or other solutions rapidly.

Give yourself a time limit and a clear plan of specific steps to take. Don't obsess over which solution is best. Pick the ones that are a good match for your energy levels and needs. Accept if you are struggling and be kind to yourself. Getting through the day itself is a success: everything else is a bonus.

Know that no solution is likely to be ideal. Instead, play the law of averages: if you try something and don't get anywhere after a given amount of time despite your best effort, then move on. Keep asking Allah for his help and keep talking to him especially late at night, conveying your concerns and updating him on your progress. It will help your mind to calm down and keep focussed on the solutions.

5. If still no joy, then start back at the beginning and persist. Every time, say Alhamdulillah for the problem, then Bismillah as you set out.

Be prepared to accept it if you don't get anywhere. The only thing we can really control in life is our efforts, from moment to

159

moment. We cannot control the result. You might believe that offering to sell off an old watch worth £10,000 for a very cheap £100 would be easy, but if it is not in your destiny, you will not succeed. And if it is in your destiny that someone was looking for that watch happens to see it and offer you £100,000, then nothing can stop your destiny either. You have no way of knowing.

You keep trying, and accept failure or partial success. Keep saying alhamdulillah for whatever you have, knowing that God has given you exactly what you need right now, and he is fully acquainted with your situation.

Many of the greatest people in the world struggled for many years, penniless and alone; some of our greatest prophets even died penniless and in pain. Yusuf (AS) was thrown in jail for a number of years for an unjust reason. He emerged to eventually become king of Egypt. If he, as a prophet of Allah, endured such issues and came out of them in the end, what is Allah telling us about Yusuf for?

Know that you have to keep moving, keep hope alive, and keep cheerful. These elements are part of your Akhlaaq. The Rules of Akhlaaq is about how you conduct your affairs as a human. Your 'Rules of engagement' as it were. Life becomes easier if you are unswayed by the deceptions of triumph or disaster: neither is a definition of you. Rather, your true definition is in trying to do your best. The results will come if you stick to that. And if they don't accept that Allah has every reason to hold you back from something you think you want, and something will show up to guide you. Keep your eyes open, and your smile certain.

Exercise: Solving Problems

Start by saying Bismillah, and by writing out a worry about a current real problem:

My worry about a current problem:

Now follow these steps:
1. Find the real issue behind the worry.
Find the underlying issue that needs fixed. Don't be too narrow in thinking about the possible solutions. Work through these questions to help you.

What is the current situation?

What would you like the situation to be?

What is the obstacle?

Define the real underlying solvable problem in one sentence:

Step 2: Create a goal or two.
Goals are SMART: specific, measurable, achievable, realistic, and timely.
They can also be short term or long term. Try to be as specific as possible. Make sure the goals fit the problem.
Goal A:

Goal B:

Step 3: Create possible solutions.
Lots of ideas, look to get inspired, thank Allah, smile and be playful, talk to others who might console you, don't feel alone, get ideas from anywhere. Ask Allah for help to be more creative and imaginative like you once were when you were an infant, learning to walk and talk. Keep your strengths and resources uppermost in your mind: you will do better using what you already have if possible.

Solutions:

Goal A:

1

2

3

4

Goal B:

1

2

3

4

Step 4: Pick which solution (s) to go with.

Now it's time to choose a solution. For each potential solution, ask yourself the following questions.

1. Do I have the ability, time and effort?
2. How do I feel about this solution?
3. How long should I give myself before changing strategy?
4. Is this the best of my bunch? If so, alhamdulillah, let's do it.

Step 5: Implementing a Solution and Assessing Its Effectiveness

With the solutions, write out literally the next steps, step by step. Could be as simple as 'go to the bank' or 'check my email for half an hour'. Go through each step systematically. Focus, move on, get through. Expect anxiety. Expect that some solutions will fail. Don't expend too much effort on it or exhaust yourself. You need to remain alive and sane. Nothing is worth losing your mind or health over. Enough is enough; its time to smile again no matter what.

Thank Allah for your problems, and for the chance you have to work on solutions. Keep an eye open to opportunities that could transform your life for the better.

Many of the greatest things human beings have ever achieved came from a time when we were in a crisis. We humans have a way of dealing with crisis that is quite polarised: on the one hand, it breaks us and embitters us, and on the other hand, we have come out of other crises even better off than before. It's not about luck or ability or being immune: it is about trying to find ways to match up to the crisis once you have accepted that everything great, even contentment, comes from humble and steady efforts every day, and difficulty is a sign that you are doing something worthwhile.

Self Care

Just like a car or bicycle needs maintenance, your mental health benefits from maintenance too. It is not enough to just expect your brain to get through life unexamined or uncared for. Just as much as you would not go through life without washing your hands or taking care of a pain in your back or knee, we ought not to neglect the most influential organ of all: our minds.

One part of self care is about treating illness and issues. The other part is about building a resilient and thriving life. This is mental wellbeing: it is more than just about 'not being ill'.

It's a bit like the damaged knee again: you treat it by medicines or physiotherapy or surgery, but you look after your body in other ways by watching your diet, keeping fit, and doing things that ensure you are functional even if your knee is hurt.

So what makes for good wellbeing? Here are five main components of good wellbeing.

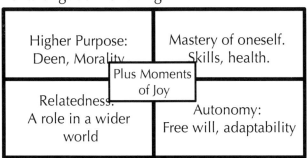

This subject is tackled much more deeply in Instant Actions. They are not about anxiety. In fact, the factors of good wellbeing can be built up by anyone whether they have anxiety problems or any other mental health issue. Wellbeing is not the opposite of illness: it is mostly separate to it, but and having good wellbeing can and does help people with many illnesses, from short term sickness to serious long term diseases, to live far more pleasant lives, dealing with their problems far more effectively.

Reasons to build a rich and varied menu of activities in life

Wellbeing is somewhat about knowing and remembering things that make you multi-dimensional. That is, things that can give you moments of meaning and a sense of value or pleasure even if you have unpleasant or difficult things going on. It is about putting your eggs in different baskets, so to speak. Hardship in one place need not hijack your mood altogether: there are other things in your life where you can go to feel good, even for a few moments.

What things do you do that are pleasant, fulfilling, enjoyable, and kind to yourself?

Some people enjoy exercise or going for a walk, others like cooking or baking, others like reading or conversing with their friends or respected elders. The ingredients for a 'full' life are basically a variety of things, different for each person, but they all seem to revolve around the ideas in the wellbeing boxes.

Having three or more of the wellbeing boxes under good control is a good formula to ensure that even if you do have anxiety, that you still attend to other things that signify a full life. Just as much as someone with a heart or skin problem doesn't drop everything because of that issue, neither should you feel less of a person, or that you have been kidnapped by your mental health problem, unable to move on until you fix it. You can and must exist in parallel, alongside your mental health issues, a full person who has desires, hopes, and a sense of your inner strength which you ALWAYS feel valuable for. You are entitled, and encouraged by Allah himself, to seek out moments of joy in your day that perk you up, however small. It is through these many routes that you can hold on to your essence.

Think of your capacity for stress as like an empty dustbin. As you go about your day, bits of trash start to fill the bin up. You would benefit from emptying that trash out because it doesn't happen automatically: you need to specifically cordon off time for your mental health. Trash must be emptied into different sections: plastics, glass, cardboard and what have you. In the same way, our mental stresses are defused by doing different things which all take a bit of that stress away.

Salah is one such a time, and nobody can ever take that away from you. Salah is your time to talk to the ultimate therapist- Allah himself- and feel that you can get out of your daily worries for even a few minutes to the sweet obligation of needing to talk to your maker.

When you have a lot of things that are stressing you out, we all know that we start to overlook the things that help us feel better. We rush through salah, we skip that nice catchup chat with the neighbour, or that video-game session with a friend.

This is fine to do from time to time: never believe anyone who says that you should always be doing certain habits or you can never be healthy or well. Nonsense. We are very adaptable and resourceful creatures. We can go through many difficulties and perils without losing our wellbeing, but there is a line that we might cross unknowingly at first, when we sense we are just giving up too much of our wellbeing. Everybody crosses that line.

Whether you become ill or return from it unscathed is not for you to know: life treats us all differently. We all get frazzled; even those of us who never admit it. We need to claim ourselves back.

Work is never more important than mental health. Other people's needs can wait until our needs are fulfilled, if we are struggling. Other peoples' *wants* should *not* supersede our needs.

Get a diary, or use your phone scheduler. Surprisingly, not many people, even doctors and healthcare professionals, know about the real principles of mental wellbeing. Most people think it is the absence of mental illness: it is not that. It is having parts of your life that enrich your humanity and propel you to be closer to Allah in the end, regardless of illness or any calamity.

It can feel a little unfamiliar to start doing things to consciously make our lives more rich and fulfilling, and pencilling in these things is a good way of trying to wedge them into our otherwise less colourful lives.

Many worriers neglect their own care, or they spend their time serving their worries in place of actually looking after their truer, richer life. This needs attention and care.

Hence it becomes important to identify the gaps in your wellbeing boxes and take steps to find things that fill them up, scheduling these things in week by week if you must.

It may sound odd but it works. I have helped a fifty year old man, a salesman off sick from work due to medical issues, find happiness again just because he started to schedule in a Sunday afternoon to contact his brothers and sisters. This was the 'relatedness' box that we fixed.

All his siblings lived in different towns and countries, but technology helped him to re-establish that contact. His relationship with his siblings blossomed like never before. He was even able to help them out, because he offered to send them things they couldn't get in their own country. He ended up talking to some of them every day. It did him a world of good and reminded him of who he once was, and propelled him back to health, giving him the motivation and energy to power through his very difficult OCD problem too.

He felt less defined by the problem, and more defined by the sense of having a life with different aspects, different sources of good feeling.

Exercise: Identifying and Scheduling Self-Care Activities

Here are some categories of self-care activities you might consider, along with examples in case that's helpful. Try to write down activities in as many categories as possible.

Your autonomy: your independence, fitness, and freedom. Physical activities. Gym, walking, running, gardening, sports, stretching. Options and ideas:

Relatedness: Social activities. Specific time spent with friends and loved ones for the sake of their company. Shopping, visiting, walks, doing something to help them out.
Options and ideas:

Mastery: a chance to learn something new or assert your individuality. Learn a language; take on a new skill. Help someone else. Options and ideas:

<u>Meaning and Purpose:</u> A chance to connect spiritually. Time spent in nature, and religious sanctuary. Reading and learning about Islam and the prophet's history. Reflecting on the Quran. Helping out in the community. Feeling awe at Allah's creations; being in nature.

Options and ideas:

<u>Pleasurable or specifically enjoyable things for you.</u> Time to savour small things, enjoy laughter, a favourite place to eat, a favourite book to read or film to see, arts or crafts that are fulfilling, games and amusements.

Options and ideas:

Now take a calendar such as the one on the next page and see if you can schedule in these kinds of things to happen at least once a week.

Activity	Mon	Tue	Wed	Thur	Fri	Sat	Sun
Fajr time	Read English translation of Quran				Read English translation of Quran		
Morning						Learn to restore furniture	Help at Masjid recycling p
Lunchtime							
Afternoon	Gym			Gym			Walk
Evening meal			Online course:: furniture restoration		Eat at Karim's. Invite Shakeel.		
Night						Facetime brother	Facetime parents

Looking at this sample calendar, you can see that one of each category of self care items is included.
Autonomy -gym, exercise.   **Mastery**- furniture course   **Relatedness** facetime & volunteering,
Spirituality reading English tranlsation of Quran   **Joy** dinner with Karim's with Shakeel,

Long term approaches to a strong mind

<u>a) Deep, mindful Salah.</u>

Salah is an opportunity to connect with God and go to an 'exclusive sanctuary' with God in a way that other people think of expensive tropical luxury escapes. Despite their expenses, their spas do not give them a direct line to the Lord of All Creation! Salah does just this, and try to think of it this way. It is an opportunity to feel as if you are being watched, loved, appreciated, protected and listened to by Allah, five times a day. As an exercise in physical and bodily relaxation, it is also excellent,. Move slowly, gracefully, breathe slowly though it, pray with attention and humility, and give all of your attention to Allah 's greatness especially in sujood.

Find the 10A's of Amazing Salah is on my YT channel, over three short episodes. Search it up and watch it to remind yourself and understand what I mean.

Link here:
https://www.youtube.com/watch?v=260M4gWaS8Y

<u>b) Exercise, activity, and nature</u>

Exercise is a strong way to flex your emotions out of your body by using up that energy you have which would otherwise make you tense.

The Nafs is bound up with the physical body. When we are tense, we notice how the whole body is affected: stiff muscles, sweating, nervous jitters, and what have you. This is a sign that the body needs to be exercised. When we do this, the result is that we release tension. Physical exercise has a natural way of

173

calming the emotions. We end up feeling relaxed because we have given the body a physical workout.

It is astonishing how well an hour of exercise, or a long walk, or some vigorous pastime, even cleaning and tidying, will do to give the body, and therefore the Nafs, a sense of having achieved something. It burns off that excess tension. Look at the animals: their entire lives are spent running, flying, swimming, escaping, searching. The Nafs is designed for a very physically active life.

For some, this might be achieved through housework. For others, it is running, swimming, riding horses, and archery (favourite pastimes of the Prophet PBUH) or going to the gym. For those less able, even a walk for 20 minutes three times a week is a great method to settle the emotional body, releasing the energy and calming the Nafs down substantially.

c) Nutrition and fasting
Provided you are in a fit state to do so, restricting your access to food is beneficial to your emotions and your thinking because it frees you up from the tyranny of hunger and concern about food, and gives your gut a break, allowing more free energy to be used by your brain and liver to think clearly and clean up your body respectively.

It is sunnah to fast twice a week-Mondays and Thursdays, and you should familiarise yourself with other types of Nafl (non-compulsory but beneficial) fast if you want to do this more regularly. I will be creating a program focussed on diet and fasting too inshallah. Look out for it, or email me to let me know what you would like to include in it.

Weekly review sessions

Now that you are working on yourself, it is important to treat yourself in a way that a professional would, What does that mean?

1. Be kind, and talk to yourself with gentleness and compassion, If you couldn't do an exercise, a therapist wouldn't call you an idiot or tell you off. So neither should you.

2. Have belief in yourself and Allah. Therapists who show belief in their patients have greater success rates. The attitude of self-belief for Muslims can be bolstered by remembering that Allah made you as complete and deserving of contentment as anyone else, and therefore you have every reason to have faith that as a His creation, you can accomplish things you need to.

3. Do the sessions weekly, regularly, at a prescribed time. You wouldn't drop into a therapist session at night unannounced, and you wouldn't have the chance to just spend 4 hours on therapy because you felt like it. Have boundaries and stick to them. If issues crop up in the week, make a note of them and promise yourself that you will deal with them in the next session, or some other allotted time when you can focus on them (so-called 'worry time').

Exercise: Weekly Check-In

How anxious were you overall this week on a scale of 0 to 10?

1 2 3 4 5 6 7 8 9 10

On average, how much did you worry this week (percent of your waking day)?

0%   25   50   75   100

What are some of the topics you worried about?

Were some of your worries excessive or uncontrollable? If so, which ones?

Were there any stressors this week that might account for your worry? If so, what was happening?

If you've had more stress than usual, how did you deal with it? Did you use any additional self-care strategies?

Did you experience any of the following symptoms this week? If so, how severe were they on a scale of 0 to 10?

Feeling restless or on edge

1   2   3   4   5   6   7   8   9   10

Being easily tired

1   2   3   4   5   6   7   8   9   10

Can't concentrate, mind goes blank

1   2   3   4   5   6   7   8   9   10

Irritable or snappy

1   2   3   4   5   6   7   8   9   10

Muscle tension, headache, or knots

1   2   3   4   5   6   7   8   9   10

Sleep problems

1   2   3   4   5   6   7   8   9   10

Did you catch yourself engaging in any anxiety-related safety behaviours troublesome habits (safety behaviours)? If so, which ones?

_____
_____
_____

Overall, do you feel that your worry and anxiety were better or worse this week compared to recent weeks?

_____
_____
_____

Exercise Review
Did you practice any exercises this week? If so, what did you do?

_____
_____

Were any exercises easier or harder than expected? If so, will you adjust exercises to the point where they are not too hard or too easy?

_____
_____

Was there an exercise you wanted to do but didn't because it seemed too difficult? If so, is there a way to make new exercises slightly less challenging and more do-able?

Skills Review
Looking at all your worry management skills, do you think you could use extra practice with any of them? If so, which ones, and what could you do?

_____
_____

Setting Exercises for the Upcoming Week
Keeping in mind the exercises you did last week and any skills you might need to work on, what exercises can you do over the coming week? If possible, try to do two or three exercises weekly.
Exercise 1:_____

Exercise 2:_____

Exercise 3:_____

Date and time for next session:

The ups and downs

We can view an increase in anxiety and worry in one of two ways:

- a normal response to an extreme situation

- an extreme response to a normal situation

In the first one, anyone in your situation would have had the same reaction. For example you come home to find your house has been burgled. Anyone would find this upsetting.

In the second one, it is more to do with the anxiety within you. This is where you can chalk the experience up to a 'relapse'- which is part of the ups and downs of coming out of any anxiety situation.

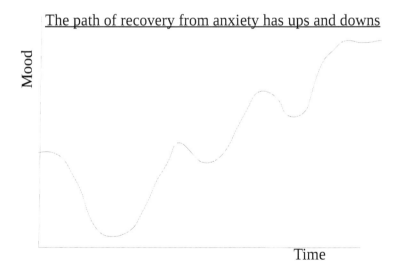

The path of recovery from anxiety has ups and downs

Managing worries is a slow but steady and very rewarding process if you keep at it humbly, and with faith in yourself and Allah. Expect things to go up and down, sometimes without any reason. Emotions are often plainly random. Missing sessions is inevitable from time to time; don't let it bother you too much.

179

Exercise: Warning signs and triggers

Everybody's Nafs is different. We each have our own particular souls. Some of us are given to seeking status and security, others with being loyal above all else, others with being respected, others with having possessions, others with being safe and predictable.

Learning about your Nafs and what its warning signs are when it is getting too agitated, is a key part of understanding yourself. When you know what is likely to upset you, you can prepare and deal with it better. It's a bit like being a weather expert: if you can see the storm coming, then you can look after your garden and prepare yourself accordingly. These are the issues that typically cause a downturn in performance. See if you can write examples of when you might notice these things.

How do you know when you are feeling run-down? Clues: tiredness, concentration, restless?

Sketch plans or ideas for what you could try to ease this if you notice it is happening:

How does your sleep change when you are having a hard time?

Sketch plans or ideas for what you might try to ease this if you notice it is happening

_____

_____

How do your habits change? What do you notice yourself doing more or less of?

_____

_____

Sketch plans or ideas for what you could try to ease this if you notice it is happening:

_____

_____

What do you notice about taking care of your five signs of wellbeing? What do you stop doing?

_____

_____

Sketch plans or ideas for what you could try to ease this if you notice it is happening:

_____

_____

How does your approach to Deen change when you are struggling? (Clues: spending excessive time in masjid or prayer, or avoiding prayers, etc).

_____

_____

_____

_____

Sketch plans or ideas for what you could try to ease this if you notice it is happening:

_____
_____
_____
_____

What do other people notice about you when you are having a tough time? Ask a couple of people what they think.

_____
_____
_____
_____

Sketch plans or ideas for what you could try to help you forward if it happens:

_____
_____
_____
_____

Review recommendations: Every 3 months.
Look over these notes every 3 months or so.

Next time and date to review: _____

Note what is going into your body

We eat, drink, and absorb information, attitudes and assumptions from the lives we choose to lead and the people whose company we are in. All of these change and influence the way we feel.

We are different in how sensitive we are to these things. Some people are totally unable to manage caffeine; others can have 10 cups a day without an issue. It is up to you to discover or consider things which may be not so good for you.

You can work out if things affect you in a straightforward way. It takes roughly 45 minutes to an hour to respond to food which we have eaten. So we can design a simple monitoring system.

This is only a very short look at food: I will be producing a program for people who want help with food and diet inshallah.

I have put this part in here because of how often people forget that what they eat or drink can cause or worsen anxiety.

Doctors don't subscribe too much to the more faddy nutritional trends, and neither are doctors convinced about the need for vitamins and supplements if the person hasn't had a blood test to prove they are deficient in it. But there are certain things which have clear impact on mental state: caffeine, sugar, nicotine, routinely low fluid intake, and sensitivity to allergy-causing food are the ones to look out for.

Tea contains caffeine too: about half as much as coffee does. Coffee is OK in up to 5 cups a day, but of you are sensitive to it, even one cup can cause emotions to become wound up.

Exercise: Food monitoring

Before I ate/drank Anxiety (out of 10)	What I ate/drank	1 hour after I ate/drank Anxiety (out of 10)	Comment

Notice Your Intake of Information

Smartphones can dominate our lives. The trouble is that they have multiple functions, so you can't say that they are truly bad or truly beneficial: they can be both those things, and many things in between.

Our smartphones. As something that is both incredibly useful and also incredibly troublesome if unmanaged, the phone resembles our own minds. They sit in several places between the line of very useful and very troublesome. This is why it is so important to limit our interactions with our phones to those which are more helpful and calm, rather than emotional and lurid.

The phone is a tool of amplification: it will speed up our development or accelerate our demise. Sometimes it helps us out in one part of life while damaging another! Better to not be so dependent on any such tool, lest we lose ourselves in it further.

The main cause of anxiety from smartphones and apps is our difficulty in *limiting our involvement* with them.

This happens because phones can help us administer our lives, inform ourselves, communicate with loved ones and even improve our lives in some ways by connecting us to Deen and reminding us of salah times, and being sources of information about interesting or amazing things. So the Heart and the Intellect find a ready ally.

But they also appeal to the Nafs, providing ready access to quick 'hits' of what the Nafs responds to: wealth, amusement, misfortune, lust, new things, gossip, gambling, and a wish to be seen as popular or strong. Each one of these causes a short, sharp increase in dopamine- the 'quick reward chemical' in the brain,

185

which then drops sharply again, causing you to seek more. This can feel like addiction without you even knowing or admitting it.

So, what do we do?
Being always connected is unhelpful to mental health. The Nafs becomes worn out and bitter, lurching from one urgent matter to the next. We dearly need to experience our natural selves, alone. Why would this help?

- We can just experience the value of silence.
- The volume of chatter in the mind is turned down
- We learn the value of delaying immediate gratification and rising above short term temptations which hijack our day.
- We can see things from a higher, wiser perspective. Imagine what the view of earth is like from a million miles away.
- Our quieter strengths get a chance to come out
- We can re-evaluate and review our intentions and aims
- We can get away from emotionally draining media.
- We improve our timing and adherence with Salah, food and other real-world obligations.

This is essential for Muslims to experience. We can start it right away if we make a decision about one thing: whether to have our phones switched on, or near us, in Salah. You wouldn't take your doorbell with you when you pray salah. So why take your phone with you? It will only ever distract you. There is no emergency that can take over your life that salah will prevent you from attending to.

In Salah, we escape to a beautiful, protected sanctuary. With one takbeer (saying Allahuakbar) we enter a place that is entirely reserved for us and God alone, at His invitation, free of guilt.

Leave your phone in a safe place away from your body when in

Salah.

Leave it off more than on. Let its default position be turned down rather than always buzzing and beeping.

Leave your phone alone in the extremes of the day. In the first hour when you wake up, and the last hour before going to bed, it is better to not look actively at the screen,. Set alarms and listen to calming du'aas by all means: use things which aid restfulness, but don't do anything that makes you interact with the device at those times when your Nafs is more dominant.

Have a 'phone box' for family gatherings. If you are sitting together for a meal, or in the lounge, make a rule that everyone must put their phone in a box nearby for the period when you are all supposed to be paying each other attention. It is not prohibited to look at the phone, but there could be a benign 'fine' system. Maybe someone who has to get their phone has to put a dollar in a jar every time they do so.

Social Media are a separate and more intense source of problems and benefits. Much of our engagement with the Ummah in COVID or in general now is through social media, but the Nafs is very socially sensitive, and strong emotions can get evoked when a person feels personally invested in anything social. Even people who are normally very sure of themselves can end up feeling insecure, unduly elevated or rejected by messages that flicker their approval or disdain alternately through the day. Perhaps one day we will get a hold of this beast, but for now, better to not spend too much time in the lion's den.

Self Test: Media and Smartphone anxiety

This is an intense week when you will be cutting down your use of your phone by a significant level.

Have a look at these statements and click how much you agree.

Thinking about your social media apps: facebook, whatsapp, tik-tok, snapchat, etc:

• I feel jealous or judged when I am using these options to communicate
     1   2   3   4   5   6   7   8   9   10
Not at all   Very much so

• I lose time every day by spending more time than intended on the sites.
     1   2   3   4   5   6   7   8   9   10
Not at all   Very much so

• I get genuinely angered at the posts that some other people make
     1   2   3   4   5   6   7   8   9   10
Not at all   Very much so
• I get jealous or intimidated by how some others seem to have great lives.
     1   2   3   4   5   6   7   8   9   10
Not at all   Very much so

• I get agitated if I can't get on a site to see what's up
     1   2   3   4   5   6   7   8   9   10
Not at all   Very much so

Look over the scores. What do you think this says about how much you are the driver or the passenger in your dealings with social media?

Exercise: Smartphone detox.

Take action to balance out smartphone dependence.

The following is a list of techniques. Pick the one (s) that appeal to you. Commit to do them for the next week and then review. At the end of every each day during the week, review how you have done in each area, and then start the next day afresh. Finally, after a week, reflect on how the week has gone.

• **Limit your availability to your phone other than by phone-calls. Tell family members to contact you by ringing you only, if something is important. Otherwise they are to assume that you will look at whatsapp and other comms as non-urgent.**
Can you do this? Yes/no

When you can start?
_____
What problems do you anticipate?

_____
_____
How will you get past the problems?

_____
_____
• **Protect the extremes of your day** when your intellect is not fully awake. Wait to check your messages for at least an hour into your workday. Try getting some work done first. Put the phone away an hour before bed, unless it specifically relaxes you.
Can you do this? Yes/no
When you can start?
_____
What problems do you anticipate?

_____

How will you get past the problems?

• **Make 'phone only' times.** Add 'phone hours' to your weekly schedule, perhaps three times a day. This gives you three full hours to deal with your phone in any day- a generous amount but probably less than what you have been doing up til now.
Can you do this? Yes/no
When you can start?

What problems do you anticipate?

How will you get past the problems?

• **Protect your food and salah times.** Turn off everything at home that rings or dings, including cell phones, while at at salah or eating. These are 'protected times'. Put the phone physically away from you.
Can you do this? Yes/no
When you can start?

What problems do you anticipate?

How will you get past the problems?

• **Remember your Akhlaaq (character) is on show.** Make it a rule to ignore notifications or buzzes when talking to anyone else face to face. You will appear pleasant and attentive to them.

Can you do this? Yes/no
When you can start?

_____
What problems do you anticipate?

_____
_____
How will you get past the problems?

_____
_____

• **Leave your cell phone in the car** when you go into a social venue, or put it on silent, not vibrate, so that your attention is completely on your companions. Borrow the plan of friends who pay a fine if they break the rule.
Can you do this? Yes/no
When you can start?

_____
What problems do you anticipate?

_____
_____
How will you get past the problems?

_____
_____

•**Respect your home life, privacy, and dignity**. If you work from home, make a specific agreement with your employer or colleagues (or yourself) about exactly which hours you are expected to work. **Don't** respond to messages from work except during those hours.

Can you do this? Yes/no

When you can start?

_____

What problems do you anticipate?

_____

_____

How will you get past the problems?

_____

_____

• **Be kind to your attention. Don't overload and confuse yourself.** Don't work or browse the phone when also watching TV or reading. Don't work while also trying to watch a program or talk to those with whom you live. You will spend less time getting the work done and will get more benefit from the relaxation.

Can you do this? Yes/no

When you can start?

What problems do you anticipate?

_____

_____

How will you get past the problems?

_____

_____

Once you've selected one of these techniques, try it for at least a week.

Repetition Recommendation: Every six months. Try two weeks free from smartphones per year. This is best done at the start of a holiday period. The detox really recovers your dopamine levels and reconnects you to the real world, alhamdulillah.

How often will you be doing these?

Which weeks will you next do your smartphone detox?

_____

_____

Supplementary form: tracking your anxiety levels day to day through the detox.

	Morning Anxiety level /10	Evening Anxiety level /10	Comment
Day 1			
2			
3			
4			
5			
6			
7			

Aadatul-Tarkeez: The habits of wisdom

The Arabic word Nafs is derived from the word *nafas* which means 'breath' or 'moment'- the shortest amount of time possible. What an apt word to describe the emotional mind: it is momentary, and deeply connected to the breathing and the sense of a short moment. It can move through time rapidly, shifting you to imagine things from the past or future, often inaccurately. It is a blunt instrument whose priority is speed rather than accuracy.

This is a big clue as to how to get in touch with the Nafs: through the breathing and senses. The Heart: your True, more mature self, is able to do so but you need to learn how to guide it. Salah and dhikr are powerful ways of focusing your mind, but we learn them as children when our Hearts are not fully mature, so we don't get the real idea of the best type of salah- a meditative, deep experience. Salah offered with deep insight and reflection of Allah is more valuable than 'mechanical' salah.

Fortunately, the Heart is also our conscious self, our 'mind's eye'. We can regain command of our attention away from the Nafs.

To do this, we can practice outside of Salah or inside. The next exercise is focusing on practice outside salah, with one target: our breathing. We have described how the Nafs is connected to the body's organs; scientifically, the emotions are rooted in the base of the brain, with connections coming and going via nerves and hormones, to and from the physical body. Breathing and heart rate are a good indicator of emotional state: the faster they are, the more likely the emotions are activated, aroused in some way.

Bringing your body down from a state of physical tension is a sure-fire way of tackling anxiety too. You may not know how tense you really are: the mind and body have a way of putting up with tension if it's there for a long time, making it seem normal.

On the other hand, people with hypochondriacal anxiety (fear of being ill) become extremely sensitive to any physical signs, mistaking aches and pains as signs of something very serious like cancer. This can be very distressing too, and it is important for us to be able to bring the body to a state of being loose and relaxed, and to ba able to live with normal aches and pains without attributing them to terrible illnesses. Either way, it makes sense to work out how tense you are to begin with.

Slowing the breathing or heart rate down can influence the emotions to calmness again. Equally, getting rid of excess energy in the muscles will also work. We will look at some techniques. To begin with, we can do a self test.

<u>Self-test: How tense are you?</u>

Click which tension signs apply to you:
Background long term anxiety:
- Abdominal pain (often reported by children)
- Chest pain- central a small point, like you can point to it.
- Dry mouth or difficulty swallowing Headaches
- Muscle tension (neck, upper back, lower back) Holding your breath
- Muscle weakness
- Fatigue
- Trouble concentrating
- Restless sleep

Do you have any of the following symptoms of social anxiety?
- Blushing
- Sweating
- Heart palpitations
- Shaking hands or knees
- Quivering voice
- Nausea

Immediate or intense anxiety:
- Rapid heart rate
- Shallow breathing
- Digestive upset
- A feeling of choking.
- Sweating
- Shakiness, trembling
- Dizziness

Even if you've clicked just 3 or 4 from this long list, you could do with gaining some relaxation techniques.

Muscle Relaxation

Have you every seen a sports coach giving advice to a professional? Many of them give one bit of advice in common: reduce your tension. Find a way to be loose and relaxed. That way, your performance is improved. You are more attentive to the things in front of you, and less caught up in theoretical worries.

When combined with slow, deep breathing, this exercise works through the Nafs again, by tapping into the muscles this time.

Your Nafs did the job of making you tense. For whatever reason, it felt justified in alerting you, and so it was preparing you for a threat. You can thank Allah for the Nafs: sometimes it is right, and at those times, it helped you out. But sometimes it gets in your way, and you need to relax it because it is stuck in an anxious state.

Tightening and relaxing muscles on purpose has the effect of regaining control over your body lowering that high-pitched tension all around you, lowering blood pressure and bringing the breathing under control too. It takes time. Say bismillah, look forward to just giving it a try, and don't worry if it works or not. Just have a go. Nothing is achieved without a bit of practice.

Exercise: Muscle relaxation

The first few times you try this it will probably not work so well. Your body is a strong force to reckon with. But persist and you will find that over time, you can relax yourself at will, which also means you deal with real-world anxieties more calmly in future. Your resilience goes up.

Take a seat, or stand, anywhere. Doesn't matter as long as you can take a minute or two to yourself. Say Bismillah, and look forward to the exercise. Don't worry about getting it right or losing your place. Just have a go.

1. Start with your slow breathing. Fully in, and fully out, with a slight pause in between, at a slow and comfortable pace. Work from head to toe. Tighten each muscle group whilst you are inhaling, and release it when you are exhaling.

2. Start with the eyes: close them tight for the whole inhale, then release. Then the jaw: clench, then release. Then the shoulders, the upper arms, the hands, the chest, belly muscles, thighs, calves, then the feet. The last group is the toes.

3. Keep your breathing slow and steady throughout, ensuring you are breathing fully out and in, at a slow pace.

4. PAY ATTENTION especially to the feeling of warmth that comes when you relax any muscle group breathing out.

Tip: Imagine a Noor (warm light) returning to your body with each breath. Be thankful, say alhamdulillah for each moment.

Exercises: Deep Relaxation Techniques

Stage 1. Deep breathing technique.

1. Stand in a relaxed way.

2. Brings your hand, or both hands, to rest on your belly or lower chest, as you would in salah. They are there to sense your breathing going in and out. Hands tied in the front as they are, across the belly or lower chest.

3. Empty your lungs of air. Now you are ready to start the proper calm breathing process.

4. Breathe air in through your nose. Let it fill the lungs evenly and steadily, starting at the bottom, letting your belly expand, and moving up to fill the top of your lungs.

5. Feel and sense what is happening ion your body: you should feel heavier and more relaxed, like a camel's belly filling with water. This is how calmness flows into you.

6. Exhale slowly, slightly slower than how you inhaled. Imagine blowing on a candle flame enough to move it but not extinguish it.

7. You can pause between the inhaling and exhaling if you like. Just make sure that you pace it, and that you don't get blue or dizzy. It should feel controlled and comfortable.

8. Once you've found a steady pace in 3 or 4 breaths' time, count out how long your inhaling and exhaling takes. Make a note of it.

 Use the table over the page to compare this pace with the pace when you are next anxious.

	Time it takes when practising.	Time it takes when I am anxious.
Inhaling		
Exhaling		
Pausing in between		

Now set 5 alarms on your phone, to practice deep breathing for at least 2 minutes, five times a day. A great place to do so is after salah to begin with, and then when you get the technique down, you can do it where it will have an intense and amazing effect: in your salah, itself, while praying your surahs, where it will deepen your concentration and help you to feel very spiritually calmed and connected to Allah, inshallah.

Stage 2. Sensing.

Ultimately, Nafs also means 'this instant', this moment. To truly be conversant with your Nafs, you can begin to try to feel everything going on around you at any given moment, and just note it. A good way is to scan your body: start with the feet, and imagine a light shining on your body, slowly moving upwards, sensing the feelings from each part the light is shining on.

This is while you are doing the deep breathing. It is harder than it sounds.

When you reach your head, you will have a number of senses to pick up: the taste in your mouth, the sounds you hear, and finally, the thoughts in your mind.

The aim is to just 'feel' these things without any need to wish to change them, even if they are unpleasant or distracting. This teaches you that no fear or emotion can really hurt you when you are calm and detached from it, and that everything, especially life on earth, is nothing but a temporary thing, a collection of senses and memories.

Once you reach this state, people report a great sense of inner contentment and detachment from the petty difficulties of the day, and the trivial nature of man's preoccupations, his jealousies and rivalries. It sets the tone for your finest character to come shining out of you.

Stage 3: The Muraqabah

Muraqabah means 'observation'. It is the word given to the Islamic practice of 'being present to the moment, and noticing Allah's magnificent creation around you'. It is a deeply satisfying state. There is no prescribed method for it; indeed, many scholars think of it more of an attitude than a technique, but many others choose to enhance it by doing deep breathing, or during their tasbeeh when they are chanting Allah's name in their mind or under their breath.

You can try this yourself. As you do, try to pace the word 'Allah' or Subhanallah' to fit in to your breathing. The more successful among you will even be able to detect your own heart rate after a while, and you can pace your words to a slow heartbeat too. Allah.. Allah.. Allah..

The effects that you have started are as follows:
The mind will begin to relax more.
The gut will feel rested, and resume digestive processes.
The blood pressure will drop to more normal, even levels.
The heart rate will slow down to a more normal pace.
Your body enters a state of being 'satisfied' and unthreatened.

Tips and hints:
1. **Seek the Noor (light).** As you breathe in, you could imagine your body being filled up with light. As you breathe out, you could imagine sins and other worries flying out of you as you think about Allah.
2. **Be joyful.** Do this in a deeply grateful state of mind. Thank Allah for the chance to think about him, and to understand yourself. Thank him for any of the blessings you have in life, and also for the problems. Let him know that you understand the ultimate truth: that problems and difficulties are part of life's many opportunities to grow as a person, and to win Allah's pleasure by showing our finest character through hardship.

Breathing technique for rapid tension relief

Increasing the amount of CO_2 in your blood tells your body that it must conserve oxygen, and it will do this by slowing your mind down and slowing your heart down too. This brings calmness more quickly if you are in a tense state.

How do we achieve this? We make the exhales (breathing out) longer.

1.Start the deep breathing process as normal.
2. On the first exhale, let it be the same length as the inhale.
3.On the next exhale, take one second longer.
4. On the third exhale, inhale for a further second longer than the second one.

You are slowly lengthening the exhaling times each breath, to a point you are comfortable. Again, don't go blue or dizzy.

The blowhole. When you are very tense, or angry and want to let out steam:
Take the deep breath in, and then blow out in short, huffy bursts-Huh-huh-huh-huh! Like a boxer makes when he is throwing punches. Do this 3 or 4 times, in a private place: it's not particularly quiet, but it is extremely effective in blowing off anger or other extreme emotions.

Shifting your focus

Anxious conditions hijack your attention, dragging you towards fears and thoughts which are false, exaggerated, or simply beyond your control anyway. Trying to reason with them sometimes doesn't work because you are just giving them more attention by doing so.

So one way to reduce them is to move your mind away from them: effectively, to turn your head away from where they take you, and look at something *you choose* to focus on.

This will achieve two things:
1. You strengthen your Heart- the true, free part of your mind
2. You learn that anxiety gets its strength by convincing you to look at one thing, and that moving away from an anxiety lets you see how small, exaggerated, or untrue that thing is in reality.

You practice moving your mind's eye to where you want to move it. It works by giving you back the control as to what you choose to focus on.

This technique is for you if you have panic, social anxiety or general anxiety.

Exercise: Shifting your focus.

1. Sit comfortably with your eyes closed. Say Bismillah, and thank Allah for your ability to sense things around you.
2. Be aware of the outside world. What do you notice through your senses- hearing, touching, temperature, weather?
3. Shift your focus back to your body. Take care to focus on how it feels to draw breath in and out. Pay attention to the movement of your chest and body, and the feel of the air passing through your nose.
4. Go back to pay attention to the external world. What do you notice through your senses again?
5. Prepare to open your eyes by becoming aware of light coming through your eyelids, and then gradually allow your eyes to open. Bring your attention to the next activity that you plan for your day.
6. Move on with your day.
7. Don't worry if you are not fully successful. Existing with our Nafs is a slow, life-long negotiation which we learn gently and steadily. It is a marathon, not a sprint.

The Nafs is a time machine. It can transport you to any moment you choose, making it seem real. You can go back to the past, or imagine some kind of future. The trouble is that the Nafs is also connected to emotions, which cloud the truth to a negative end. Your Heart can bring the Nafs back to the present time: the only time which we have any hope of controlling.

Special Worry Technique

If you have worried so long that you are something of an expert, you might as well treat it a bit more professionally. Give it times slots, keep a boundary around it, that sort of thing! Read on to see how this makes a surprising amount of sense.

Anxiety is all about excessive worry. It can be realistic, or unrealistic, but there is too much of it to handle. So, is there a way to help worries along by a bit of reverse psychology? By giving worries the space they demand, can we reduce their volume?

There is wisdom in this path. Two reasons why it might work:

1. Most unpleasantness from worry is when we fight it. This is exhausting. If we just let it flow and give it some special airtime, it might settle down. We might have the energy to actually deal with it more sensibly afterwards.

2. Worry is *noisy.* By giving worries special time and place to pay it attention- essentially, a bit like calling worries over for a cup of tea at 7pm, then we can clarify the worries and give them the sense that we understand they are part of us.

3. Think of worries as unpleasant, needy guests. If unpleasant needy guests are always arriving to visit unannounced, wouldn't it be smarter to give them an invite for a special time? That way we know when to expect them, and we can hear them out more calmly. We've gained a bit of control back, and we can work with them to help them out

So, the next exercise is about these using these techniques.

Exercise: Special Worrying Technique

Start by saying Bismillah, and thank Allah for giving you the chance to overcome a difficulty. Whether you succeed or not is not in your hands. The only thing you have to do is have a reasonable try.

1. Set aside a specific time tonight, or later in the day or week. The first session should be up to two hours, no longer than that. After that, sessions should be about 30 minutes, ideally toward the beginning of the day. You will be writing, or making notes, or even just thinking things through. That is your 'worry time'. It can be the same time each day.

2. When the time comes along, start by listing all the things you could be worried about. Dissect the problems.

What are the worries about?

a._____

b._____

What could go wrong with them?
a._____

b._____

Why are they a concern anyway?

_____

_____

3. Now make a PLAN of ACTION that you don't have to act on right away, but is just a list of CONCRETE SIMPLE FIRST STEPS towards solving the problems. If the problems are not there yet, make a plan of what to do if and when they occur. It could include making a phone call, talking to someone, finding information, any action that will move you towards your goal in the smallest way.

Problem a:

Step 1._____

Step 2._____

Step 3._____

Problem b:

Step 1._____

Step 2._____

Step 3._____

4. If you have enough time, then get on with those steps.

5. Ask yourself, "Is there anything else I need to worry about?" Your brain needs to hear a "no." If you say yes, you need to redo steps 1 through 3.

5. If you have run out of time, then you need to wait until your next worry session to continue.

6. At your next worry session, continue with the plan and the solution, right from where you last left off.

7. If the worry crops up in between worry sessions, then thank it for coming, but tell it that it is invited to the next worry session where you will give it full attention. That way it will be treated with greatest attention, and not be rejected to wander about and hassle you when you have other things to do. It has an invitation to come to a meeting!

8. If the same worry crops up again, kindly tell it that you have already worried about it last time, and that it can come along to the next worry session if it likes, where you can go through the same solutions to help it along.

Additional technique: The Worry Box

1. Imagine a box. A pleasant, wooden box, very tough, with a nice door on top which opens up. It can hold all of your concerns. You can put whatever thoughts you like into it.

2. Now, make a quick list- just a few words or headings, about the all the things that are pressing on your awareness or asking for your attention. Anything —good or bad, big or small—can go into the container. Give each thing a name.

Example 1: I might fail the exam...

_____

_____

3. When everything has been named and put in the box,

a) accept that they are part of your mind, and you have found a place to store them for now.

b) thank Allah for the worries as they are, and for providing you with the box to contain them.

c) Set the box aside in a shelf or place that is safe in your mind, or imagine a place in your house where the box can 'stay'.

4. Ask Allah to help you to get on with your day. Get on with your next things to do. Invite your Intellect and Heart to come along and help you with your day now that you have settled the emotions in a safe place. They can help you focus.

5. If you are stick for ideas, go and make wudhu, and pray two rakats salat-ul-Nafl as thanks for Allah's help. Pray with great gratitude and optimism that you will get through this and that peaceful good ideas will come back to you.

6. At night time, you can remember what was in the box in your du'aas, and talk to Allah in du'aa: ask him for help in managing the

209

box, in soothing the worries and promising to open the box to look at the issues when you are ready to deal with them at their appointed time.

7. When the box is opened at a time of your choosing, you may well find that the worries have diminished in size, or indeed disappeared, all on their own. Such is the power of this technique. If no change, that's fine too. Proceed as planned with your plans and solutions, in your worry time. Keep it separate and honour it as ling as the worries are still lurking.

Perfectionism

"If I do this right, without any mistakes, then I will have no need to worry", and so go the beliefs of someone doomed to worry forever.

Contrary to popular belief, many worriers and many people with anxiety disorders don't see themselves as perfectionists. They see perfectionism as a method to ward off anxiety. This is, of course, not going to work out, and Allah is not pleased with people who try to imitate perfection: a quality reserved for Him alone.

We are designed by Allah to have faults, doubts, imperfections and inconsistencies. He is pleased by the process and effort we make to overcome difficulties, and how we correct our mistakes and learn. He never expects us to be perfect: we made that assumption all by ourselves. And that itself becomes an exhausting and damaging problem.

It comes back to not watching the Nafs again. The Nafs is naturally driven to compete, have higher status, to ensure everything is as it wants it to be. This is useful only in moderate amounts. Beyond that, it becomes an unachievable quest for the impossible.

We are, in truth, valuable and loved by Allah even if we achieve nothing. He cares not for our achievements but for our character.

Allah wants us to have a life of relative ease, of reasonable effort. Perfection will always evade us, and should never have been our aim in the first place.

Competition between each other is natural. It has a ready place in the Nafs, therefore competition doesn't need too much invitation at all before it shows itself. It might help focus the skills, but competition is a slippery slope to combatting others and isolating oneself. To achieve truly great things, we collaborate, not compete.

Imagine two people at College. There is Jamil, who is just born with good maths ability. He doesn't need to study for a test, and gets an A without much effort. Then there is Musa who struggles, studying very hard for days on end, and gets a C. The school might reward Jamil, but who Allah reward more? Musa. Allah will still reward Jamil if Jamil shows good character and spends his time in something constructive. Allah cares about our intention and our beliefs, not our achievements as such.

So instead of perfection, we aim for *excellence*: *trying our best*, not *being* the best. And not overdoing it, because we would otherwise bring harm to our body and mind. Doing a reasonable job is far superior in mental wellbeing than trying to do achieve perfection.

Perfectionism is founded on a fear about our beliefs about ourselves and our appearance to others. We mistake perfection as a marker for the quality of a person's inner values, but in reality, such a person is probably quite troubled and finds it difficult to be with their own mind, let alone other people.

So, we can set about trying to identify our own perfectionism.

Self Test: Spotting our own perfectionism.

• Do you make du'aa asking for all problems in your life to be solved and to never have any struggles again?

1	2	3	4	5
Almost Never				Very often

• Have you ever been blamed for being too 'controlling' or bossy, focussing more on the results at the expense of how people feel?

1	2	3	4	5
Almost Never				Very often

• Do you take on extra work because you feel it is 'just part of your personality' and then felt overworked?

1	2	3	4	5
Almost Never				Very often

• Do you believe you would have more fun and good times in life if you could only find the time?

1	2	3	4	5
Almost Never				Very often

• When you are responsible for making something good or pleasant happen, do you feel unsettled or a lack of pleasure, despite the fact that it should be a fun thing?

1	2	3	4	5
Almost Never				Very often

• Do you work until you are totally worn out, almost unable to even move and with no idea when you will get going again?

1	2	3	4	5
Almost Never				Very often

Look over your answers. Where do you find yourself leaning towards? The Nevers or the Oftens? For those completely untroubled by perfectionism, it would be Nevers all the way down.

The questions are deliberately a little vague, to make you think about yourself. If you find yourself getting a little annoyed and arguing with the questions' validity, that itself is a sign of perfectionism!

Let's look at it a little differently. Write down some answers to the following questions.

1. I believe in trying to get the best outcome for the people I love and work alongside, whether socially, at work, or in matters of community and Deen. How do I show that?

----

2. I always try my best and would never intentionally try to underachieve. I am prone to be hard on myself, much harder in judging myself than I do other people. I do catch myself calling myself an idiot or a fool. Here are some examples:

----

3. I believe the details are where most good things can set themselves apart, or fail. I pride myself in noticing and caring about the details of things. Here are some ways I catch the details of things:

_____

_____

_____

_____

_____

_____

4. It is hard to know when something is good enough, compared to when it is perfect or amazing. I try to get to 'amazing' because I believe it is only a tiny bit more effort to get from 'very good' to perfect'. Here is an example.

_____

_____

_____

_____

_____

_____

Exercise: Addressing perfectionism.

Emotionally, perfectionism is often connected to anger and a wish to be in control. Many people gain a perfectionist streak because they may have felt unable to control things when younger, and the wish to correct that and find a sense of inner peace is driven by a deep but understandable frustration. Perfectionism is a way of defending against that horrible anger. It is not as bad as being always angry, but it is still tiring and negative. It had its place, but has outlived its usefulness: it needs to be let go.

Letting go of that anger and fear is sometimes the key to releasing oneself from perfectionism's grip. Forgive and move on from things or people who upset you, even if they don't deserve it. Why? Because you deserve peace.

If you answered yes to even some of the questions in the last exercise, perfectionism is getting in the way of your life. Don't panic or even worry a bit. This can be easily dealt with if you believe you want to change it.

Here are some things you can do.

• Have greater faith in other people. Delegate something to others, even if you feel they might not do it as well. Examples: cleaning, cooking, budgeting, organising something.

If possible, how could you try this out in your life over the next week?

• Listen to when other people use 'always' or 'never' in their speak. Life is very rarely 'always or never'. This is called absolutism, and is a close cousin of perfectionism. Absolutism only really works when

216

trying to motivate the Nafs to action: certain pep talks and inspirational speeches with their strident language, are designed to stir the Nafs, using symbols of grandiosity and immaculate victory. Perfection and absolutes are only possible with infinite time: if you are immortal, go ahead. If not, then re-examine your language because it could be reflecting troublesome thought.

Try to remember a time when you were trapped in perfectionist thinking. 'All or nothing', Victory or Defeat' 'No second place'.

Did it get out of control? How did it feel being trapped in that space? What advice would you give yourself now, looking back?

• Do you believe that extremely good results are ONLY achieved by perfectionism? Have you noticed how some truly high achievers make it look easy? Maybe they trust in Allah and get better results because they are less tense? If so, then you might do better when you are less tense. Tension and perfectionism are business partners. Can you leave that partnership and maybe achieve better results by trying less intensely?

Aim for non-perfection. Other people must be happy with you doing your best. You must be happy with trying your best, rather than what you achieve.

If it's not life-threatening, be happy to doing it imperfectly. See if others can tolerate you as Allah does: as an imperfect being. If they can't, then understand that Allah accepts you even if other people don't. And if perfectionism is the norm in your chosen activity, think about how the really high achievers seem more relaxed.

If possible, how could you try this out in your life over the next week?

217

Observe the work of someone who's easy going and seems not to be too fussed about things. When they do something 'good enough' how do other people respond? If you were seeing them with the eyes of someone merciful and generous, what do you enjoy about the way they are?

More notes on perfection: now set yourself some aims and activities.
On this date or in this situation:

I will do these things:

Reviewing the situation:
Did anyone care whether I was perfect? Their names are

If something went wrong unexpectedly, how did I and others cope?

Can I tell the difference between the consequential things and inconsequential things?

What are my thoughts about what Allah expects from me? Am I able to be more imperfect, like he planned, or is something holding me back, keeping me tense? Can I try letting that thing go, for the sake of Allah.

EXERCISE: Getting round too many jobs to do.

Make a list of all the things you need to do. Spend half an hour, really belting the list out, from small to big. Now, look at the list, and separate them out into these categories

A. Urgent and Important

B. Important, but not urgent:

C. Urgent, but not important:

D. Not urgent, and not important:

Now employ this strategy *aggressively:*

219

For A: Do them now.

B: Postpone them for later on.

C: Delegate to someone else

D: Drop these altogether.

Don't put your livelihood or safety at risk, so if something really needs done, do it. Otherwise, it can wait, and see how well you can tolerate the wait. Discover how little everything really matters, compared to your own sanity and being happily imperfect in Allah's eyes.

End of program words and reflections

Thank you so much for having a go. Good results, though pleasant, are not as important as the honour of trying. I hope you keep trying to be as kind to yourself as Allah would be. Treat yourself with dignity and forgiveness. Be OK with messing up. We are not made without a purpose. Being alive is proof of that.

Thank Allah for bringing the program to your attention, and thank him for however much progress you have made, whether huge or small. Allah knows and sees all, and loves his servants immensely. He loves it when they put effort in to help themselves or others to overcome problems.

Deen has prime place in mental health

Belief is protective against pain and suffering, and belief allows one to take positive risks in life while accepting the possibility that things might not work out. Sometimes, people's mental health problems get caught up within their religion too. This program will help with that part too, inshallah.

All of deen is about how we behave. All of faith resides in what we choose to believe.

It is no surprise that so much of the Quran and Hadith is about instructions, warnings, and examples about how we are and how we should aim to be.

All of this is to do with our minds. Our humanity is a wondrous cloak, hung off the hook of our ability to think, believe, feel, and act. Without the mind we are lost. We would amount to no more than a collection of organs with no reason for being. The eyes would be globes of soft clear tissue, the lungs spongey bags, and the heart merely an interestingly shaped muscle. All would be

221

disunited and meaningless. It is the mind which navigates life; all other organs serve to help the mind achieve its wishes.

To have a clue as to the importance of your brain, look at where Allah has placed it. On the highest location of your body, away from the hard earth. Surrounded fully by hard bone, with the bone at the top of the skull being the most rigid and strong of all our bone mass. Surrounded by protective organs of sight and sound.

And to signify our humility before Allah, look at what we do. We pray Salah, isolating ourselves from the world around us, vulnerable, and we place our heads on the ground to demonstrate our most precious possession is at Allah's mercy and for his worship.

So maybe that explains why mental health is so seldom talked about. It is because we all fear the possibility that the most important organ of all is somehow not doing its job properly. We laugh at madness due to fear of it in ourselves, rather than true humour.

The brain is also difficult to understand scientifically, more than any other organ. We can be simple creatures in some ways: we believe that if we can't see something wrong then it might not be real. It is a silly thing to think of mental illness as not real or believable because we can't see it. Like believing that planes cannot fly because we can't see what is holding them up in the air.

When I was at medical school, I learned that most of the basic functions of the body's organs had been discovered by the 1940s. The heart was a pump, the guts are a large expanse of absorptive material, the lungs are spacious sponges for air to be exchanged.

The brain, though: we have not had the technology to look at it, because a microscope might be good enough for other organs, but doesn't tell us too much about the brain. Today's technology allows us to see which parts of the brain are active when we think about this or that, and how subtle changes in the tiniest substances can affect the balance of wellbeing and happiness in a person.

Once in medical training, I was learning neurosurgery alongside a famous professor. The patient, remarkably, was awake, and through a hole in his skull the professor was removing damaged tissue while asking the patient questions. The point was to make sure that nothing essential was being damaged by the surgery. The patient being awake was a key part of the strategy of safety.

At one point, the professor was kind enough to alert the patient that he was going to teach me something, then he touched his blunt forceps on an outer part of the man's brain. The patient's arm moved upward, and the patient himself was surprised: he didn't intend to move his arm. The professor had just touched the part of the brain where the movement of his arm was controlled. And so began my understanding of how the mind is an organ like any other, and my mission to try to help people to think and feel better, combining my knowledge of the mind with the unseen, invisible knowledge we have about the spirit, the psychology of people, and the way the mind functions over and above its strange physical shape.

To put it into context, science will still take time to catch up with what Allah had designed in our head.

Psychology and psychiatry are very scientific, but they are not very technological. Asides from some neurosurgery and other new techniques, most of the work we do still relies on medicines and talking therapy. But there is nothing wrong with this: we are exercising the mind when we talk and think, so it follows that if we talk and think in specific special ways, we can train the mind just like we train a muscle in the gym after it is injured. We can and do correct many problems with this approach, and just as you would see the muscle grow if you trained it in the gym, we can see physical changes in the brain's functioning and chemistry when we have treated a psychological condition properly.

Alhamdulillah, anxiety disorders are among the most common but also among the most successfully treated conditions that affect the brain. Many of these techniques were discovered first by some Islamic teachers above all others. The world's first psychiatric centre was in Baghdad, founded by a great physician called al-Razi. Talking therapies, healing potions, nutritional approaches, exercise and other programs were all practised there.

Islamic thinking about the mind is incredibly deep and detailed, and actually quite compatible with modern medical knowledge. Those old doctors and philosophers of Islam knew what they were doing, and more to the point, the Quran and Hadith had laid down the excellent foundations for them to base their practice on. This remains true today, and will remain so for all time. While medicine evolves and changes, the Quran and Hadith have no need. Instead, we discover deeper wisdoms in them as time passes, exactly as Allah himself predicted in his words in the Quran. Let us become ever wiser in understanding them as we pass through time, Ameen.

This advice, whether you find it in an app or a book or online, is very helpful to inform yourself, but if you can't get along with it don't blame yourself: after all, if your brain is struggling you will find it difficult.

Remember to be kind to all of Allah's creatures, and that includes being kind and merciful to yourself. Treat yourself as you would someone very special and important to you: you are your own an employee, very valueable to your future, starting work on their first day, every new day.

Be unafraid to seek help. Consider it a fardh to look for help if you can't manage on your own, because your body and mind are only LOANED to you by Allah. He has commanded you to look after them. It takes courage to reach out to someone, to look at ourselves and to make changes. Courage is available to anyone who believes that Allah is truly with them for anything good they set out to do.

Dr TK Harris MD

Muharram 1442 AH
September 2020

INDEX

Other titles by Dr TK Harris

Instant Insights: The Muslim Mind Guide for Contentment and Success in testing times.
Discover how the mind works and what makes for success in *Deen and Dunya*. What goals are worthy? How do we start doing things which make us more masterful of life? All is revealed.

Instant Actions: A Training Manual Using Islamic Insights to Fly Strong Though Change.
Instant Insights put into practice. More than 38 common situations where we can do simple things to uplift ourselves, not just for quick gains but for lifelong changes. Relationships, organisation, conflict, career, and a whole lot more.

Voyage of the Humble Soul: You were born with wings. Go on a journey to Perfect your Flight.
More than 200 people were asked to give their thoughts on how they experienced Hajj. This is the story of Zed, a young man who returns to Mecca for the first time since childhood. He has dreams, visions and meets inspiring people along the way.

All books are available in multiple formats, including audio, paperback, and e-Book.
Go to **drtkharris.wordpress.com** - the central source of all titles.

Or, search for the written titles on Amazon.
Find the **audiobooks** and some new written releases on Dr Harris' Etsy store.
https://www.etsy.com/uk/shop/drtkharris

Forthcoming Titles

Tharwatul Qalb Series: Interactive Self-Guided Programs

Tharwatul Qalb literally means 'Wealth In the Heart'.

Future Volumes of this series will be separate programs covering:

- Effective Weight Control, Fasting and Nutrition
- Successful Investing and Financial Life
- Defeating Addictions and bad habits
- Success after Trauma
- Depression and Bipolar disorders

All profits from sale of books and media go towards making this app and creating more free-to-access media.

Tharwatul Qalb: The APP for Android and iOS.
The Ultimate Muslim Mind Kit.
Build a Strong Mind using interactive games, quizzes and challenges.
- Achieve your Goals in Life and Deen
- Find and maintain worthy goals
- Succeed at hime, work, study and career
- Manage and defeat mental health issues
- Improve relationships and happiness

This comprehensive Mental Wealth App is currently in development. It is expected to launch in late 2020/ early 2021.
It will probably cost a modest amount to start with, to help complete its development.

Follow me on Instagram @drtkharris to keep up with this and other developments and get access to free media.

231

Youtube Channel: Mental Wealth with Dr TK Harris
For all playlists go to youtube.com/c/drtkharris

A series of short videos covering all themes to make a Strong Muslim Mind. Techniques and knowledge covering a wide range of topics in mental health and wellbeing.

Season 1: Introduction to the Muslim Mind.
A Doctor Marries Religion With Science.
Combining Neuroscience With Religion
Why Am I So Emotional, Doc?
Why Do We Over-React?
The Intellect Explained
How To Improve The Intellect.
Finding your True Self - Your Heart.
Understanding The Strong Muslim Mind

Season 2: Building a Strong Mind.
Hang on part 1- Courage and strength for those in crisis
Hang on part 2- When things start to look up.
Akhlaaq: an introduction to its power
Akhlaaq pt1. Powerful life truths.
How to build excellent character (akhlaaq)
Self awareness: a doctor teaches techniques
How to make du'aa for a strong mindset and self awareness.
A doctor explains prayer.
How writing and speaking improves self awareness.

Season 3: The peaceful mind.
How Muslims Find Inner Peace.
Introduction To OCD And was-was (Intrusive Thoughts)
"My Thoughts Won't Stop!" A Doctor Explains How To Deal With This Problem. Ocd, was-was, Anxiety
Unwanted Thoughts: Cure For Ocd & was-was
Defeating Unwanted Thoughts. Ocd And Islamic Medicine
Salah Pt 1 Secrets Of Praying Deep, Mindful Salah. Scientific And Religious Method. Doctor Explains.
Salah Pt 2 The 10 A's Of Amazing Salah. Improve Your Salah Using Neuroscience.
Salah Pt 3 Neuroscience Applied To Muslim Prayer.

Printed in Great Britain
by Amazon